BEAUTIFULLY REDEEMED

Angela Rodgers

To Carmen
B Blessed

BATTLE PRESS
SATELLITE BEACH, FLORIDA

Painfully Broken Yet Beautifully Redeemed

Copyright © 2021 by Angela Rodgers

Painfully Broken may be ordered through booksellers or by contacting:

Angela Rodgers
www.Angelamrodgers.com
Contact@Angelamrodgers.com

Or:

Battle Press
steve@battlepress.media
www.battlepress.media

ISBN: 978-1-5136-8277-8 (SC)
ISBN: 978-1-5136-8278-5 (eBook)

Library of Congress Control Number: 2021905095

Photos on back cover "Memories to Love by Laura Ann". Courtesy of Laura Bolling.

Printed in the United States of America.

First Edition.

Contents

Dedication

To Myke, my soulmate. I have failed in a lot of things but finding you again in 2007 was not one of them. Thank you for picking up my broken pieces and just holding them until I could put myself back together. I love you.

To my children, I have messed up in a lot of ways on this journey. Thank you for forgiving me when I could not forgive myself.

To my Mom, Thank you for not sending me to boot camp when I painted your carpet pink. I pray to be ½ of who you are as a person. I am who I am because of who you are. I love you mom.

To Jeff and Teresa, We are forever bonded by this ugly circle called grief. Thank you for offering me grace when I did not always give it back.

To Jamie McGuire, Thank you for Travis Maddox and our Beautiful Friendship with my Disaster self. I am forever grateful to you. You are as real as they come, and I am blessed to know you.

Disclaimer

I have tried to recreate events, locations, and conversations from my memories of them. To maintain their anonymity in some instances I have changed the names of individuals and places. I may have changed some identifying characteristics and details such as physical properties, occupations and places of residence.

There is no time limit for grief, and many things can leave you reeling and spiraling out of control. Still, the intensity of grief tends to lessen with time.

If your grief gets worse over time instead of better, or interferes with your ability to function in daily life, consult a grief counselor or other mental health provider.

The publisher and the author make no guarantees concerning the level of success you may experience by following the advice and strategies contained in this book, and you accept the risk that results will differ for each individual. The content in the book all come from the author's recollections, though they are not written to represent word-for-word transcripts. Rather, the author has retold them in a way that evokes the feeling and meaning what was said.

Special Thanks And Acknowledgements

Sometimes dedications are just not enough. My story was very much formed, helped, and supported by so many people.

Cathy S, Thank you for being the pink diamond to his titanic. You will forever have a piece of him with you. We will forever be bonded by that "damn dog".

Barb Birchmeier, Thank you for keeping your word always with my boys, even when the table turned.

To My "Jesus" Sisters, You all know who you are. Thank you for not giving up on me when I wanted to give up on myself. Thank you for holding my hand when needed and loving my not so loveable self at times.

To Billy P, Thank you for teaching Jarred that his past did not define who he was. Thank you for always answering my calls but not always answering his. You taught me some hard lessons on tough love. But I can honestly say that your mentorship of him in the 12-step program helped greatly. Taking him to the club to go to meetings and to hear you speak helped me be able plant the mustard seed of faith he grasped onto finally. You taught me the phrase "Keep on Keeping on". I to this day still say that daily. You, Coco, Kane, Emma, Harley, and Luke hold a special place in my heart and always will. Thank you for keeping up the good fight. Emma, I love you kiddo, so did he, remember what he told you.

Finally,

To Pastor Paul and Jessica, Thank you, for asking me twice to be part of your "Faith Family". Your love has made me a better mother and us a better family. I would not have made it thru this journey without all your love, guidance, and faith in me. Thank you for allowing me to be part of your team. Pastor Paul, I do not think you ever knew your direct part in my faith journey. Now you do. Thank you for reaching into my soul, speaking to me, and filling me with the word's that I needed to hear. You did the same thing with Jarred and I know that in the light of his eternity that is what mattered. Jessica, words cannot express my gratitude to you. You hold me accountable with love, when needed. Thank you for your friendship.

About the Author

Angela M. Rodgers is unapologetically a lover and teacher of Christ. This relationship was fortified even greater as God restored her through the deaths of her two sons. She is a native of Michigan and enjoys her country living with her kids and husband. Angela and her husband have adult children, grandchildren, and dogs but equally important she has been the foster parent of more than 50+ children. Even in all that Angela is a preacher, Court Appointed Special Advocate (CASA) volunteer and works to rescue women who have been victims of sex trafficking. Angela is a fierce advocate for children and this type of advocacy is only birthed out of true adversity. She is not afraid to share the raw and personal details of her tragedies and grief in order to help others understand the redeeming and healing love of God. Her testimony is her healing. Her testimony will be the catalyst to your healing as well. As a normal everyday woman and mother, Angela seeks to share her journey of grief and redeeming love of God with you and others. She does not have any fancy titles behind her name or degrees, but she has a powerful story of resilience, faith, grief and surrender that is delivered both with humor and bluntness.

Preface

Painfully Broken Yet Beautifully Redeemed gives practical guidance to help break the Destruction of the cycle of Grief and Faith. This book is a true story of the life of the writer and her family. It begins with what was a Non-faith-based approach to how she handled the Grief of her stepson Jacob's murder, which was one of the roots of destruction in the home. Angela then explains a Biblical version of the same grief when she got the opportunity to have what she calls a 'Do-Over' when she loses yet another child named Jarred just 2091 days later. It is all here in this trying, sad and eye-opening exploration of the biblical principles on parenting, grief and how to live again after loss. This book can help make families function as God intended for them to function, even thru the tragedy of death. Grief does not have to steal the life away of those living. This is a personal story, and any information contained herein, is for the sole purpose of information. It is the writer's personal story. It is her family's personal story as seen thru her eyes. It is what led them to faith and led them to what they now believe as their complete Savior and Redemption with the Lord Jesus Christ. Not many people can say that they received a Do-Over like this. It is an incredibly sad but true way of looking at the deaths of two children at the age of 19 and 18.

Chapter One
My Genesis

When I graduated from a Catholic High School located in Ann Arbor Michigan I thought I had life figured out. Little did I realize I didn't know anything. I was a broken little girl, who had zero faith, in fact I rebelled against anything that even tangled with that word. Given where I went to school this was ironic, especially since it was a Catholic high school where you are made to eat, breathe and live faith.

I honestly thought I had the rest of my life ahead of me, I thought that I was indestructible. You see, I was brought up in a Blue-Collar family and my mom and dad were fantastic parents. My dad, although a recovering alcoholic, died with 26 plus years sobriety under his belt. I have two older brothers; Robert and Kevin, and I was my dad's baby girl, nicknamed "Ding". My mother worked a lot in the community with at risk youth, and my father retired from one of the big three car manufacturers and loved to bass fish. I was not born with a silver spoon in my mouth, but looking back I definitely had it better than the foster kids I take in today.

I remember growing up with thick burnt orange shag carpet on our floors, along with the big box TV. You know the ones that have the 8-track tape and record player in the top of the cabinet. Our water was rust ridden because we lived on the lake. I was at times embarrassed to have friends shower at our house because sometimes water came out of the pipes a copper color. I have fond memories of spending Saturdays at the laundromat with my mom. Mom and I would wake up and go to the laundromat where I was able to play a few video games, Donkey Kong was my favorite, and Pac-Man was and still is my mothers. Often we would eat lunch together. We as a family did not have the most expensive or best of things, but we had everything we needed. Funny, or ok not so funny story about my mother, God bless her soul. We just had new beige carpet installed in our living room, no doubt after a huge amount of planning by my Mom and Dad. I was a speed skater at a local Roller Rink, and my skates were Jet-black with the bright orange wheels complete with black trucks and neon bright pink laces. I decided that I wanted to spray paint the skates pink. I mean, this sounds like a great idea so far doesn't it? So, I went to the shed and got a box, then broke it down and lay it flat on the carpet. I laid the skates on the box, and spray painted them pink, but I did not account for the "overspray". My dear mother now had pink tinted carpet right in front of our big brown box Television. I am honestly surprised that I did not get sent to "boot camp". My mother was just the type of person who offered so much grace even when it was not deserved. I am not saying she was not mad. I remember her standing in the kitchen at the Island the next day, I literally saw her do this as I was watching an episode of "The Dukes of Hazard" while sitting in the Living room. Just speaking of this I am getting the butterfly feeling in my stomach and thinking to myself, "O crap, I'm in so much trouble" I remember looking up and seeing Mom tilt her head to the right with one hand on her hip and saying, "Is my carpet pink"? "Why is my carpet pink Angela Marie?" "Ummm, yeah about that mom, "I'm sorry."

I remember my mom taking my best friend Jamie and me to a name brand store and buying the first pair of name brand shoes and clothing I ever had. Little did I know the planning it took for my parents to afford this. I felt like the luckiest girl in the world. I do not know what was better, the Guess jeans she bought me or the water softener that her and I both loved having as I became a teenager. I will say that I was happy with both. Looking back at it now, as a parent I totally understand the dilemma of having to pick and choose your battles with your kids.

My parents did the best they could raising us. I was blessed for sure. We had our share of dysfunction, with addictions in my household. My father stopped drinking when I was about seven years old. My brothers had their battles as well, as did I.

At the end of the day, I was really protected from a lot of what took place. I also spent a lot of time at my grandparents' house. The choices we made were just that "our choices". I know as children we often disappointed and crushed my parents. Heck, to be completely transparent, as adults I am one hundred percent confident that we have all crushed them a time or two.

My brothers paved a very transparent way for me when we were younger. Let me just say that growing up they kept things interesting in our house. I honestly could not get away with anything if I tried. Because by the time my parents survived my brothers, they had seen it all.

I remember one instance when I was younger. I was out with a friend and decided it would be a great night to test my Mother's connections with law enforcement in our community. I am not sure why I decided to do this, as she was generally a step ahead of me. In fact, most times she knew before us kids even got home what we did, with whom we did it and what trouble it caused.

One time I decided to test the theory and stay out all night. Mom was able to track me down, in fact telling the police officer that they better beat my father to where I was at, or it may be a different type of 911 call coming in. My father was a small man, but he knew how to handle himself if needed; especially when it had to do with me. If he did not handle it there was always my two older brothers who were willing to. I will tell you I was more worried about my father getting a hold of someone I stayed out all night with instead of the police. After being punished, I never stayed out all night again.

Looking back at my childhood, I can honestly say that my parents failed our family in one way. When I say "failed", I will also say it was not "intentional". They did not raise us in a home of faith. Therefore, one huge difference is I had no foundation of a religious belief because I was not brought up with one. I suspect you are thinking to yourself "She was not brought up with faith yet went to a Catholic school." I did not go to a Catholic school, I was sent there, not because I was Catholic, but because I was failing miserably in our Public school system. I was beginning to leave a trail of mass destruction. I was failing, skipping and about to fail out completely in my junior year. It was not necessarily by choice, it was out of necessity to graduate and walk across a stage. Little did I know that the stage would end up being in a church where communion was given prior to my getting my diploma.

If I could go back and change this, I definitely would not. I learned more in one year than I did in three years attending public school.

I spent most weekends with my grandparents growing up, they lived near Willow Run. I idolized my grandparents. My grandfather and I would spend time in the barn with our horses, and my grandmother and I would go shopping and bake. Looking back on it today I smile with the memories.

My grandfather and I were remarkably close, he always handled himself with such respect and dignity. My grandmother was a trip. She was bipolar and was a lot of fun to be with. She would often wake me up at 3:00AM to have a tea party. Looking back now, I realize she was experiencing mania at times, as a child I just thought she wanted to have fun. I still remember the tea pot she used, and the little triangle sandwiches she made with slices of cucumber and mayonnaise, however mine were straight peanut butter and jelly. Another great thing was I didn't have a bedtime curfew when we stayed at our grandparent's house.

My grandparents went to church every Sunday, and on the weekends when I stayed with them, I went also. The church they attended honestly scared me a bit at my young age. It was a Pentecostal church that did things differently than Catholic churches. Now I know the difference in the churches. I am in no way saying that the Pentecostal faith is bad, my oldest niece Niccole follows Pentecostal faith.

I remember people praying over me as a young child and feeling like something was wrong with me. One time I was in the middle of a group of people who at that time seemed to be speaking a foreign language. As they were touching me I recall feeling scared. No one explained to me what was taken place. I began laughing and wondering what in the heck were they saying and what was wrong with me. Full disclosure, I am the type of person who laughs when someone gets hurt or at the most inappropriate times. Not because it is funny, that is just my armor. My grandfather was so upset with me that day. I didn't get my cinnamon ice cream treat from Bill Knapp's. Back then, this was a big deal. I remember another time being counseled alone by the pastor and him patting his lap and saying, "Little Angela Marie come sit here with me so we can talk," as he patted his lap, which I thought was very weird. Nothing bad ever happened, it just did not feel right to me. I never told my grandparents about this behavior; in fact it is likely that they didn't even know.

Looking back as an adult, I feel like I was being groomed. It was at that point I decided I did not like religion or believe in God. My viewpoint at the time was "If faith feels like this, I don't want it."

I have never grasped the reasons for the behaviors I witnessed, I just knew it was not for me. I still did not understand the word faith. I now realize that they were speaking in tongues which was a gift. But that was not my cup of tea at the time.

Around the age of 16 I was introduced to an alternative "religion" called Wicca. It was different, appeared powerful, and honestly looking back was one of the biggest mistakes of my life. I practiced Wicca for many years. That will be another book at another time. I do not want to go too far into this because I won't take away or scar my son's stories. There is a quite different, painful, and deep story about my Wicca days that could make up a whole new series, explaining how I transitioned to Christianity and moved from darkness to light. I will say that I did a lot of things that I will never be proud of regarding the "dark side".

You may be asking yourself "What does this have to do with "Grief?" Dealing with grief begins with your foundation, which teaches you how to deal with and handle things. I am not saying it makes it any easier, what I am saying is grief is all consuming but different for everyone. You cannot just skirt around it, the only way to help yourself is to work thru it. I have personally had the opportunity to deal with grief that is unfathomable times two.

I majorly messed up dealing with Grief to the point that I lost myself, and was unavailable as a mother, wife, daughter, sister, and friend.

I will be completely honest when I say that I am surprised I am still standing today. It saddens me to say I got a "Do-Over" on how to handle my loss again. Gosh, this statement still pains me to the core of my heart. But I cannot express it any differently. I know what it is like to majorly screw up dealing with grief, and I also know what it means to be able to do it right when Jesus gives you grace and the opportunity for a second chance.

What I can tell you is that if you stick with me and read what I have to say you will have a deeper understanding about the different faces of grief and how to get off that hamster wheel that just keeps going around and around.

Sadly, it took me a long time to get off the hamster wheel myself. I can 100% without any question tell you that the difference in "self-destruction" versus "self-care" and "self-preservation" is FAITH in the Lord Jesus Christ. It is not just knowing the outcome of death is grief, it's ONE HUNDRED PERCENT trusting the process that your mind and body goes thru to begin the healing. This process sucks, but if you trust it and stick your roots in faith, instead of de-rooting, it truly does heal you.

If you are anything like me, you may want a "guarantee" to what I am saying. Most people don't want to act unless we know for a fact that what we're doing will indeed work. As a matter of fact, we want it to work for us BEFORE we put all our energy, time, and effort into it. We look around for ways to bypass the process or find a different path, but the process never changes. The only thing that can change is our willingness to trust the journey, and many times, we need to figuratively be whacked in the head before we finally get it.

Pain is a highly effective teacher, no one ever explained that to me that way. Through my pain, I have learned a great deal and have gotten so much understanding during the past few years and have surrendered to going through some processes that I was not open to before.

Trusting this process means doing the work even when it doesn't seem like it is working. I had to decide to notice it, acknowledge it, and choose that I would ACT in Faith anyway. That's trust.

Chapter Two
"Foundation"

I got married young, in fact a couple of times. One marriage blessed me with two bonus sons Robert and Jacob. They were about 3 and 5 when we got together, I was 21ish. He and I then had two children Charles and Jarred. Jacob, my stepson, was a hyper and rambunctious little boy. While my other stepson Robert was a gentle old soul growing up, a caretaker of sorts, he was my big helper. Charles was our miracle baby, it took many rounds of infertility treatments to have our little boy. Jarred was a surprise to us after going thru what we did to get pregnant with Charles. Ultimately our little surprise ended up saving my life. They found Cancer when he was born, and then came surgeries, etc.

Man, I was young, I thought I had the world in my hands. Little did I know I had no clue how to parent four young boys. I did the best I could, but I did make some mistakes. Looking back, I sometimes just shake my head. I most definitely was not the best mother then, but I did do the best I could. But I have had a lot of forgiveness to give myself over the failure to provide the proper foundation for my children then.

We lived in a small farmhouse in a small town in Michigan. We were together nearly eleven years then decided to divorce. My ex and I are now friends and have tried to remain friends throughout raising our boys. It was not always easy, and I know I have failed multiple times.

Today, I can honestly say that I respect him, his current wife, and my now husband Myke at a level I did not know existed due to the losses that we all share. We are forever bonded by the ugly faces of Grief. Each one of us had our own way of dealing with it, I can only tell my story.

I am happily remarried to my high school sweetheart Myke. We got back together in 2007. Myke blessed me with two more bonus children, a boy named Gavin and a girl named Alexys. Myke and I now also have adopted children thru foster care. I am thankful that we began our foster care journey together after we found our faith. We have tried hard to build a life that we do not need a vacation from. We also make sure that our foundation is strong with Faith.

My ex-husband and I currently live about fifteen minutes away from each other. He and my husband Myke have went hunting together, our children have shot archery together, and we have spent holidays as a family together. Like I said, it was not always nice, but healing is power. I will be honest; our lives took many turns over the years.

In fact, many derailments took place also. But I will say again, I have a new respect for both my husband Myke and my ex-husband along with his wife, because we are forever bonded in this ugly circle called Grief. At the end of the day, we have the same thing in common, we lost our boys, we loved them and we miss them. Having that common ground sucks but that path was chosen for us.

To understand my personal story of grief, it is important to understand first the family dynamic of the people of my inner circle. In understanding this very thing, it may help to paint a picture of what is yet to come, what has happened, and what needs to happen.

In looking back now, I realize I failed multiple things from the very beginning. One being the foundation I began to lay for my children, was that of the same foundation that was laid for me by my parents. I can't change that now; however I can apologize and make amends to my children for that. Which I have done. They know a different mother today with their younger siblings than they knew growing up. I can't tell you how different life might be today for my children.

There is no such thing as a perfect parent by any means. There certainly isn't a book that tells you how to be a perfect parent. There is however a book that teaches you how to be a Godly parent, and how to raise your children to be godly children. It is one of the oldest books in history named the Bible.

The bible offers four particularly important parenting lessons that I can say I failed miserably on. If I could go back and get a Do-Over with my older children, I would definitely follow the following four lessons closer:

- Be a good role model. It's not do as I say not as I do. Children will follow your example not words. Be who you needed when you were younger.
- Be unified in leadership. Parents who undermine the other, tear down your own influence.
- Build a personal relationship with your children. Children who have a good relationship with their parents will have a better and earlier relationship with God.
- Intentionally train your children. If you don't train your child up in faith, the world will train them against it.

Chapter Three
Jacob

Jacob was living in his hometown with a friend and his mother, and he had some struggles. Jacob and I did remain in contact after his father, and I divorced. He would often come and fish with my husband, go to wrestling meets to root on his brothers, and would come visit when he could. He loved animals, in fact he had a ton of them. He was a child that would let a bug outside because he did not want to harm it.

I remember one day Jacob was about 15 and we were camping at a local campground. A huge water snake came into the beach area. All the girls, myself included, began screaming and running out of the water. To us it was more like an anaconda than a small water snake. Jacob literally walked into the water, grabbed the snake, put it into a bucket and decided to relocate it to the front lake where people did not swim. I would have just killed the snake. Ok.....I would have just had my husband kill the snake, but no, Jacob went out of his way to preserve it and relocate it. He walked with his little brother's bucket in hand with a towel over it to the front lake. Which was quite a long walk. He went onto the dock and started to release the snake only to realize that it was no longer in the bucket. They backtracked and found it near a volleyball court at the campground. He put it back into the bucket again, put the towel over the snake and tried again. This time he succeeded in putting the snake back into its natural habitat without harming it. Most people would not have put that much effort into releasing a snake and just let it be wherever it was. Jacob was more concerned with the children playing at the nearby park, volleyball court, and with the snake being killed than he was with the backtracking double attempt at the snake's release.

Jacob had a love for life and everyone in it. He was a stellar 6' 4 inch, 180-pound man. I could put both of my feet inside one of his shoes. He was an athlete who loved to wrestle at his high school. He was obsessed with reptiles and exotic animals. I believe he wanted to pursue something in that line of work one day, perhaps working at a zoo.

Early April, 2012, I received a call from Jacob, he was 19 years old at the time. He called and said he wanted to come home from where he was living for Easter and to celebrate his 20th birthday that year. His little brothers and I were ecstatic because the last time he was home was a few months prior. Sometimes when our children become adults, they often don't choose to come home. So I always really appreciated it when they did.

We planned for the days and things he wanted to do. He mainly wanted to hang out with his little brothers and fish some with Myke. We discussed his menu choices of what he would like to eat while he was home. This always made me laugh because he always picked the same thing. I could count on his choices each time, but I still asked.

For one meal he chose his favorite: homemade macaroni and cheese that my late Grandma May used to make. This is not your typical Mac and Cheese, it is the artery clogging kind made with Rigatoni noodles, hand sliced sharp cheddar cheese (because the pre-shredded really does taste different), and butter, baked a golden-brown, then for another meal his traditional choice of Lasagna. Then he picked biscuits and gravy for one breakfast and he wanted waffles loaded with peanut butter, syrup and bacon for another breakfast. It has been a long-standing tradition in the family that you get to pick your choice of birthday dinner, so on his birthday he chooses to have homemade beef stroganoff, and instead of cake he wanted Ice cream sundaes with the chocolate shell coating on top. So, we finished discussing his choice of menu for his visit. I was excited; my kitchen is my home.

We chit chatted for a bit more about different things, one in particular. I remember that I was giving him some grief over his taste in music like I always had. Jacob LOVED heavy metal, the heavier the better. This day on the phone I could hear a song by his favorite band playing in the background. I jokingly said "Son, that music is terrible," he responded "It's my lullaby". I had to laugh when he said this because even as a child, he loved music. During this call he said he had been going thru some struggles of his own with addiction and some mental health issues. It really broke my heart hearing some of the struggles he was having. I didn't want to push too much during this call, I decided I would wait until he got here to finish this conversation. I just let him talk as I listened.

I remember while I was on the phone with him having a gut feeling that something was off, but I could not quite put my finger on it. As a mother how many times do we second guess our gut instincts in a situation involving our adult children? I did this day when speaking with Jacob. Would this of changed his mind on coming home a day later, likely not. But maybe had I had just a little more time with him on the phone I would have learned more about what was happening with him. Often as parents of adult children, we just take a back seat to whatever they seem to have going on in their lives at the time, I wish I had been more intentional during this call.

I was just excited for him to come home and spend Easter and his birthday with us at my mom's house. He was so tall that he was able to hide the Easter eggs up high and the kids had to climb on his shoulders to find them. So as a mother, in my mind I just went on planning the week with him.

I did not ask many questions, I just wanted him to come spend some time with us. At one point during the call, he asked me if he could call me right back, he had another call he had to take. I said yes, half expecting him to forget to call me back as our kids do.

I remember getting off the phone and looking at Myke and saying, "Jacob is coming but something isn't right." Myke brushed it off, not thinking any different. I called his older brother Robert and let him know Jacob was coming to visit, letting him know he was welcome to come hang out with us as well.

About 10 minutes later Jacob called me back. I am not sure what transpired in that call, I did not even ask for details. Jacob told me that he would be coming home a day later than we originally planned, because he was going to be with a friend of his. I really did not want to argue about it, I knew he had been going thru a lot of stuff and just wanted to see him. I told him that was fine and to be careful. He said he would and then we hung up.

I sent him a text message immediately after that said, "Not feeling good about this," he responded simply "I'll be fine don't worry about me, see you in a couple days." I responded "Love you," and he responded "Love you too."

I am encouraged that the words we shared with each other was based on love. I got to tell him I loved him, and he got to tell me he loved me as well. We had a great conversation that day and shared a lot of laughs.

Although I know Jacob knew that I loved him, a part of me knows that I could have told him more. At the end of the day, can a child be told that they are loved too much? I certainly don't believe that is true.

Today I am extremely thankful that I got to tell Jacob I loved him. I didn't know that this would be the last time I would have the opportunity to speak with him.

One thing I am 100% sure on is that when Jacob went to his eternity, he knew that he was loved. I do take comfort in this. You never really can know when the last conversation will take place, it is a blessing and a curse all in one.

Chapter Four
The "I" in Grief

The next morning Jacob was a victim in a double murder suicide, when an ex-boyfriend of his friend broke into the home and killed him, his friends' mother, and then killed himself also. My stepson died from blunt force trauma to the head with an axe. There is much more to this story, but in an effort to protect the surviving victim, I will not write any further on the crime that took place. In the matter of an instant, five families were absolutely destroyed. Mine, his father's, his mother's, the perpetrators', and the surviving friend's family.

I remember the day, time, weather outside, what was cooking on the stove, and what I was doing, when I felt my world come crashing down on me.

My boys were at their fathers for an extended weekend. In fact, that day they were at a local amusement type park. At my house it was just my husband Myke and his daughter Alexys. Biscuits and Gravy were cooking on the stove top for a late breakfast. I specifically remember being upset because I burned the bottom of the biscuits. It was raining outside, but just starting to clear up, Myke was putting some things in the shed.

I remember opening the sliding door to smell the rain. Alexys asked "What are you doing?" and I stated "I love the smell right after a good rain."

It was early afternoon when Alexys handed me the phone that was ringing, I was cooking at the time. I remember looking down at the caller ID and thinking to myself. "Great, one of the boys must be sick." I answered the phone "Hey", knowing it was their father. I heard a pause then one word "ANG" it was not just "Ang" it was more like "AANNNN-NGGGGGG". It was strangled, urgent and heart-breaking. I had never heard his voice in this tone before. I think my heart may have stopped for a moment. I immediately said, "What happened?" and I looked at Alexys and said, "Go get your dad please" as he was still in the shed. I knew something was wrong just by the tone of his voice. I then walked into my room and shut the door. I said, "What's wrong, what happened, are the boys okay?"

I did not know what it was, I just knew it was bad. I heard him take a deep inhaled breath, but I specifically do not remember him ever exhaling out loud. To this day, I can still hear this in my mind, it was as if he forgot how to breathe. The next words from his mouth still haunt me today in my sleep. "ANG, I don't know....O MY GOD....I can't.....O MY GOD....This cannot be real" I got upset and yelled at him, "What happened?" "Where are the boys?"

He replied, "Jacob is dead. O MY GOD Jacob was killed, I don't know all the details yet, but Jacob is dead." I immediately dropped to my knees. My husband walked into our bedroom after hearing a bit of the conversation and attempted to comfort me, and I lashed out. I was mean and hateful. I was just awful.

Things went into a blur, anger set in, disbelief, fear. A strong distaste for God who I did not even believe in as well. But hey, I needed someone else to blame.

I had just within a few months prior to Jakes passing began to question a lot of things that were revolved around Wicca. Also, my sense of belonging within that practice, but I still did not believe there was another way. I certainly was not looking to make a "faith" change any time soon. I had just begun to question the "moral compass" of things that I knew regarding it.

That is so difficult for me to say today. I blamed a God that I did not even believe in for taking my child away. I did not blame the act of free will of the person who killed him. At that time, it was easier to blame someone who I did not believe in than blame the mental health and free will of who killed him. At that time I had nothing better to do because I quit living myself.

I began going thru the motions. The motions of getting lost in myself, in my own pity and grief. Thru this process of grief, I not only lost myself, but I also became a shell of who I should have been and a person I do not even know. I began failing at being a mother, became a distant wife, and sadly I just felt like I died along with Jacob. Honestly, a part of me did die for an exceptionally long time. Every day was just "motions", there was no substance to any of it really. Get up, put boys on bus, go back to bed, get up and get boys off bus, make dinner, eat, put boys to bed, stay up reading all night then do it all over.

I remember the media harassing us and our young children. We did all we could at the time to protect them as much as possible. They were ruthless. Sadly, one day we were at the funeral home preparing and planning for Jacob's memorial, my son Charles had on his team wrestling sweatshirt, on the back it had his name, and, on the front, it identified where they went to school. I distinctly remember the news camera panning around to him, I saw it and stepped in front of my son, but it was too late. Pandora's Box would be opened. At the expense of what sanity my family and I had left.

It became instant insanity. Media was calling my children's school, trying to find them. News of my child's death had reached the United Kingdom and the prime-time News, including multiple pop-ular national morning shows.

It became national news without a filter or thought of protection for the family that was left behind. My son's picture, name and personal story was every-where. Details that sadly I did not even know. Remember me saying earlier, some things just did not seem right when I spoke with Jacob. There was more I did not know but was finding out thru media outlets.

During this time, the principal of their school, Mrs. Birchmeier, a great friend of mine today, really looked out for my kids, we were in almost daily contact for my kid's safety. I honestly do not know what I would have done without her at that time. She watched every door, every move they made, and even put in extra security precautions for them when they were outside for "breaks".

We had a conversation one day and I remem-ber her saying to me, "Angela, when they are here, they are in my school. I won't allow anyone to get to them, when they are here, I am their acting "par-ent". She protected them as if they were her own. My children could not even go to school in peace, the media was everywhere, but Mrs. Birchmeier made sure that them being in school was the most normal part of their day.

To this day I don't know that my children knew what was even going on around them, because Mrs. Birchmeier did exactly what she said she would do. She protected them.

What the media did not understand is that this was my child, my children's brother, my mother's grandchild, my brother's nephew, my niece, and nephew's cousin, not their "news", he had a family, young siblings, and friends. The things they were releasing about my child, we had not even had a chance to let our family know. This added so much grief to the situation that was already unbearable. Then there are the news outlets that spread lies for click's and likes.

My children never got the chance to grieve their brother, I never got the chance to grieve my son.

In fact, I think I slept for the first year of it and read. I dove into books; I found an Author named Jamie McGuire, she wrote a series called *Beautiful Disaster*. The title to the book grabbed me because I was a complete disaster myself. The book was right up my alley, I mean the name itself was me in a nutshell at that time. So, I purchased it, read it, and then read it again and again. I reached out to her one day via her site email and just explained what had happened to my son and what her book did for me. It was more of a thank you note. She personally responded, and it was the most heart-felt, genuine response that I ever could have imagined getting. Much to my surprise, she sent me a signed book. I was blessed enough to then become friends with her, not only did I find a love for her books but as a bonus I met an amazing supportive person that I still talk to today. In a way the books kept my mind busy, they let me hide. To this day around his death anniversary every April, I will open the same book *Beautiful Disaster* and re-read it. I know it almost by word now but there is just something about flipping the pages, seeing her personal note that her very own hand penned in the cover page just for me. "To Angela, know that I am thinking of you at this very difficult time." Every time I see her, I take this very same book and she re-signs it again and dates it. It has become a thing I just do. During this time, she blessed me in a way that to this day I am thankful for.

I am not saying this was a healthy way to deal with my grief, but it worked for what I needed at that time. So, I began to sleep, eat, read then do it all over again the next day. In the end I gained almost 100 pounds, I went from a size 14 to a 26 of pure miserable anger and dysfunction.

Did I mention I still had zero faith? I still blamed God for losing my son. Part of me blamed myself as well for things I did in my past. I self-destructed right before my husband's eyes. In doing so I lost so much time with my other children and my husband as well. How ironic is this? I lost Jacob which destroyed my world as I knew it, only to allow that to take me away from my other children and husband, who were alive and well and needing a mother and wife to support and take care of them.

I look back on this now and I can say. "Man, I SERIOUSLY MESSED UP." My husband Myke is my rock, and he did the best he could keeping up with everything. The fact that he did not leave me during this time still amazes me.

I can only imagine how fun it was to live within our walls during that time. Even as I sit here and type this, I get tears in my eyes because of what I put my family thru, he not only had to be a father to our four young children, but he had to be a mother as well.

My children were angry and acting out. I failed to see any of it because I isolated myself to the point that I became a prisoner in my own mind. My children in essence learned to live without their mother because I was nonexistent and unavailable to their needs. So, what I did was allow them to lose their mother who was alive and well'ish, AFTER just losing their brother.

Also, to make matters worse there was a trail of death that took place from 2009 on. We lost my father's lifetime best friend Lee, my paternal grand-parents Charles and Dorothy in May of 2009, then within six weeks we lost my father on June 13, 2009. This all took place within a 6-week time span. The level of Grief that just stacked upon itself was all earth shattering. It was like a layer upon layer of pure sadness, anger, and defeat.

People from the outside looking in thought everything was ok, in fact I heard daily, "You're the strongest person I know." No. I really was not. I was failing miserably, and my children were lost amid the chaos in my mind.

My children and I had never properly healed from the loss of my father and other family members, then got a huge blow when Jacob died. At that point I just thought that "God" liked taking people I loved because of stuff I had done in the past. That is no excuse, my children and husband needed me, and I could not even be there because I was all consumed with things in a non-biblical and unhealthy way.

Looking back, I am in awe at the grace and favor that God showed me during this time. I did not even understand it and I most definitely did NOT deserve it. But he gave it to me without me even knowing, because I still did not believe in him.

We were part of a local campground, the same one that Jacob went to with us, when he saved the beach from the anaconda snake that wanted to eat everyone alive. Ironically, it was a Christian based campground. We liked it there because it was safe and secure for the kids to roam freely. It is really amazing how God placed people in our lives that he knew we needed. There we got the opportunity to become close with the Camp director named Pastor Rob and his wife Kim. They really mentored me thru the feelings that I had during this time. I remember Pastor Rob coming to our camper and sitting on our deck and praying with me. I was still so angry over loosing Jacob. Pastor Rob shared a personal grief story with me that made me begin to look at things a bit different. I passionately believe that Pastor Rob and Kim began to open my eyes and my heart to a different way. God used this camp to begin transforming me to who I am today. Again, proving to me he had the plan already made for us all along. He placed us in the very place that my family needed at the time we needed it. Looking back now at the events surrounding how we came to know this camp along with the people there, there is only one answer to this. This was God's divine intervention in that I began to allow God to step in and change the outcome of the situation that was actively destroying me. Spending summers at this campground with my family began to change my foundation that was broken.

To be completely transparent on this, I still struggle today with **ONE FACT**, the **ONE FACT** that I absolutely helped cause in Jacob's foundation, the **ONE FACT** that I never personally had the conversation with him about, the **ONE FACT** that still haunts me in my sleep on some nights. **I DO NOT KNOW IF JACOB WAS A BELIEVER IN CHRIST AND ACCEPTED HIM INTO HIS HEART. This ONE FACT** is my fault and I take full responsibility for it. Because of this I cannot attest to where his eternity lays. You heard me right. Today, I am hopeful that he was much smarter than I was at that time in his life. I am hopeful that he knew then what I know now. This is something I will not know the answer too, until I am brought home to my own eternity.

Given the amount of time that Jacob spent at the campground with us, I do hope that there were some seeds planted with him in faith. I have learned since finding my own faith that it only takes a small mustard seed.

At Jacob's memorial it was standing room only, in fact the overflow of people were outside in the parking lot. He was an extremely popular young man, so it is my hope that given the amount of time he spent at camp with us, and given the amount of people who loved him, that someone introduced him to faith and gave him a small mustard seed.

There is a lot of bible scripture on "mustard seeds of faith." I will say that once my faith was found I did a search for it, because I wanted to understand the dynamic of what could have been for Jacob.

Mark 4:31, "It is like a mustard seed, which is the smallest of all seeds on earth."

Matthew 13:31, "He told them another parable: 'The kingdom of heaven is like a mustard seed, which a man took and planted in his field.'"

Luke 17:6, "He replied, 'If you have faith as small as a mustard seed, you can say to this mulberry tree, 'Be uprooted and planted in the sea, and it will obey you.'"

Matthew 13:32, "Though it is the smallest of all seeds, yet when it grows, it is the largest of garden plants and becomes a tree so that the birds come and perch in its branches."

Most people draw relief from Jesus's point about the power of a faith that is small like the seed. But a larger truth behind this is that mustard seeds *grow*.

Seeds have the influence to recreate the worlds around them. That's what faith does for us beginning with the world within. So there are a few things to understand when thinking this through.

- The mustard seed is living.
- It is refreshing even though it appears to be dead on the outside
- It is revitalizing in such a way that it leads to the bearing of fruit.

(Yes, mustard trees have fruit.)

Although, I do not know for sure where Jacob's eternity lays, I am hopeful knowing the possibility of the small seeds that were planted, even if unintentional.

Chapter Five
Different Faces of Grief

Isn't it crazy how many faces there are to death? But one thing is in common; each one hurts. Death, even though it comes to all, is not always the same. It comes with so many different faces.

When dealing with the death of a younger person, death wears the dark face of the enemy, an unwanted and unwelcome intruder, something terribly negative. When a person in their youth dies, we feel robbed. The younger the person is the more we feel that way. Sometimes this gives the feeling of an "unlived life". I have heard time and time again, "Jacob was robbed of his life". Was he?

On this occasion grief is bitter, even angry. Some of us have experienced that kind of death, not only is it sad, but it is also tragic; it is extremely hard to accept the death of someone that is young. But, when death comes at the end of a long life, to someone who was ill and older, death wears a quite different face. I may even suggest, the face of a friend, or a blessing per se? Death is death, Eternity is Eternity. I have spoken with people who had lived long, lived well. In the end, they were waiting for death to come, not denying its approach, not rebelling against it, they were simply waiting for their time here to come to a fitting end.

My father Charles was one of these people, I remember in his end days, he really became a shell of who he used to be. Being bed ridden and unable to care for himself, he was ready to let go and be with his eternity. It was almost a blessing to see the suffering end. He spent months in the hospital prior to his death. My mother decided to bring him home where he could be with his family and dog Lady. My father died soon after in his living room with my brother Kevin and his dog Lady by his side.

With my father I was upset, but I was in a different mental state with it. I remember being at peace with my dad's passing, but yet I was so angry with Jacob's. I remember saying "Thank God my father isn't in pain any-more." Then cursing him for taking Jacob. I was still cursing and thanking someone I didn't even believe in. Gosh, I was a train wreck mess. I was on a one-way course of collision. As my children would say today, "Mom you were a hot mess." They would be right.

As we began to notify people of my father's passing, it was the typical. "I'm sorry for your loss", "He is no longer in pain". I got this and understood it because I agreed with this. My father never would have wanted to burden anyone with his care. With Jacob, as we began to notify family members and friends, it was quite a different reaction. It came with immediate anger, resentment and hurt. I understood this as well to be honest.

We did appreciate everyone's condolences; our family does have a great support system. Looking back now, it really does go to show the different faces of grief. Both were real, both were different. However, when it begins, we know a loss puts us on a journey that you didn't ask for. This journey can change us. Isn't there a saying "What doesn't kill us makes us stronger?" I do believe there is some truth to this. But I certainly do not want to be so simplistic to that statement either.

I distinctly remember a different feeling sitting at my father's memorial then when Jacob died 3 years later. As I stood on stage and spoke on my father's behalf to a church full of people, I was not angry, bitter, or even mad. In a way I was thankful that his journey was over, and he was out of pain and at peace.

It made no sense to me at that time. Was I broken? I think with Jacob I spent a whole year in complete shock and dismay. I could not function. I remember getting the kids off to school and sleeping until they got off the bus, then I would sit and read all night so that when I closed my eyes, I did not relive the phone call "AAANNNNGGG" and crime that took Jacob. I do not know to this day if my children even knew what was taking place. Myke kept that together well at that time. Or should I say, my husband held it all together so I could completely fall apart.

Little did I know what I was really missing was just faith, and a strong relationship with the Lord Jesus Christ. Had I known then what I know now, I still just shake my head in response to that.

I began living again in about 2014. I look back now at the time I wasted living in my own self-pity. The amount of time I lost with my children and family. I can never get that time back. I had no clue how to deal with this grief that I was having or with the anger and PTSD from the crime that took Jacob. I just lived how I thought I could survive.

Regardless of which face of grief you experience or whichever way you decide to look at it. GRIEF is hard. Whether the grief is from an expected loss or an unexpected loss. The process is still a journey on an unknown and sometimes unpaved bumpy road. It is an individual journey and the path that your grief takes, won't be the same as the grief journey that someone else experiences. Offer grace, even when you don't feel that it is deserved.

Chapter Six
"The Hamster Wheel"

Do you get up every morning with the same thought about your loss that you went to bed with? Can you not eat the meal your loved ones loved? Are there certain events that trigger you? I would be lying if I said this will change, it won't but hang in there. That's encouraging right? I was recently accused of putting a positive spin on grief. One might have thought that it was meant as a compliment but, in this instance, I assure you she did not mean it as one. This person screamed at me and said something implying that my grief journey was nothing but a field covered with sunshine and daisies. I at that point had to thank this person and tell them that, even though it was not intended it was the best compliment I had ever received.

No matter how hard we try to focus on the positive, there really isn't a standard optimistic spin on that Hamster wheel of grief. We can grow, transform, and develop but grief is still grief, and it does not just let go of your heart.

However, I can say that if you cannot change your circumstances you need to change your perspective on this. It will help you feel like you can live again and not just flow thru the motions of "life".

Living again after a loss, is like playing Russian roulette with your heart. Each day is a new day that brings a certain amount of what I call the five W's (Who, What, Where, How and Why), it's like a never-ending cycle of "Who's going to bug me today and say something stupid? What are they going to say today to try to make me believe they think they know what I am going thru? How am I going to respond and not be a jerk? Why did this even happen to me?"

It is like spinning a wheel and just waiting to see where it lands. If you are going to land on your feet, or in bed depressed and unavailable for the day or for a week, or if you will lash out in an inappropriate way.

I remember getting so mad at people for the daily "How are you doing?" Ummmm, let's see, let me count the ways that I am angry and still missing my loved one. Or the "I know how you feel." Ummmm. But do you really? I think I was just salty like that at this point. No one meant any harm; they simply did not know what to say either. I mean, what do you say to someone who just lost a loved one? "I'm sorry for your loss," well no crap, I am sorry too. BUT NOW WHAT?

Let's face it, they do not make a *Friendship For Grieving For Dummy's* book...O hey, I have a new idea. I just knew that there had to be a better way, a better way to deal with the pain I was enduring, and a better way to learn to live again after losing a child.

Grief is this weird hamster wheel that you're going to be running on for the rest of your life. If you have ever watched a hamster running on those little wheels that are in their cage, it seems like it never stops. In fact, if it does stop, it is just for a moment then it starts back up again. Especially during times that you don't want to hear or see it.

I don't necessarily like the term "moving on," because loss stays with you forever. If you can't change your circumstance, change your perspective to "Grief is a privilege because it means that you had the opportunity to love someone very much." Many people don't get to have that. This may help the hamster wheel slow down.

Chapter Seven
Faith

The story of my faith begins a bit abnormal. "Clearly". Coming from a position of the "Wicked Witch of the West" to a position in "Christianity" came with its own struggles internally and spiritually. I had been going to the campground for a few years, so God was really trying to work on my heart while I was there. But it wasn't until later that I finally took the plunge in faith. I had been invited to a local church by a lady named Jessica, but I did not go. In fact, I stayed noticeably clear of anything to do with it, in fact lying to her and making an excuse as to why I could not attend. What was I going to say to her "I can't go because the church might just burn down or implode if I enter?" Like I said, I had been questioning the "Practice of Wicca" for a while now, But, I was not quite ready to try something else yet. Because let's face it, my faith was working so well for me at this point right? So I simply lied to her, "I can't come because I can't bring my kids." She gracefully smiled at me and said okay.

It was not until one day, I found myself praying to the "God" I did not even believe in over some issues taking place with my son Jarred. You see, by this time he was lost in some addiction or gang activity and was just going to end up being another statistic. I get into this more in his "Do Over". I think he deserves his very own chapter or TEN.

In a nutshell, I was responsible for his downslide because I was so lost in my own grief over Jacob that I did not see what was taking place with my own children. I know previously I cited, "our choices," when discussing my family when I was young, but not in this instance.

It was absolutely my fault that my children's foundation had failed. Did he make his own decisions? Absolutely. Did I teach him right from wrong? Yes...? But did I raise my children in faith? NO. So I found myself praying one day to a "God" that I did not yet believe in, to save my child who I never taught about God. I should have been praying for God to save me from myself. I was still dabbling with "darkness" in my mind, I was not however practicing Wicca, but my mind was still very dark.

It was a different day that I went into the same local establishment with my then younger children and I was invited to church again by Jessica. But this time she began with telling me about the children's programs they had thinking that my kids would really enjoy them. She was telling me this while I was in line to get snacks with my children. One son looked at me and said, "Let's go that sounds fun." I thought to myself, "Well played Jessica, I just wanted a darn hot pretzel with cheese sauce." I agreed to try it out sometime.

Guess what, I still did not go, it took a couple months for my decision. I knew my husband would be resistant to a new change. But one night while sleeping I had a dream of us all being in church together. I still did not go, the next week was a trying week with court hearings surrounding Jarred.

I may have also had a root canal scheduled, a haircut and multiple other appointments as well.

Because let's face it, I didn't make it a priority even after having the dream of all of us attending church together. I continued to make excuse after excuse as to why I could not, should not, and wouldn't attend. Again, they were nothing but excuses because in reality you make time for what's important.

Excuses are not reasons. Reasons are genuine happenings that keep you from accomplishing things in your life. Excuses are those things that we blame for outcomes that should have been prevented. Excuses are within your control, and reasons are not. Here is the absolute truth about excuses. Nobody else really cares about yours.

The reason I say this is in hope that it will give you that extra little push in the endeavors you have been contemplating. Whatever the case may be, the only way that excuses will ever stop is by taking the first step in the right direction.

I had to make a conscience effort to decide to take responsibility, or to continue making excuses for the foundation that I was allowing with my family. To take responsibility I had to take owner-ship and initiative to make this change in our home. This was going to be a huge change, in fact opposite to what they knew. I was expecting some resistance. But I just decided this was going to hap-pen.

That following Sunday I woke up and just decided we were going. I packed up our younger children and did just that, we went. I am talking no planning, no warning to any of them, no sitting out church clothing. Nope. Just woke up and said, "Get dressed, we are going to church." Not one of the children had a complaint or issue with getting up early on a Sunday, getting dressed and out the door by a certain time.

I was half geared up for a meltdown or two from one of my children. I was pleasantly sur-prised. In fact, they were dressed and out the door in record time.

As we took the 10 minute drive to where we were going. I reminded them of all the things I had remembered from a young age walking into a church. Behave, Sit still, etc. I must have heard "OKAY MOM," ten times during that drive. I remember pulling into the parking lot and letting out a big sigh. Was I really about to do this?

I sat in my van for a few minutes with my younger children, who were bouncing in their seats with anticipation of walking inside. Little did they know I was really contemplating turning my van around and driving back home. The thoughts running thru my mind at that time were telling me that I was not worthy enough to be accepted into a fellowship of Faith. Oh, and perhaps a little of "What If I ignite and catch fire in front of their eyes." I looked into the rearview mirror and my son looked at me and said, "Are we gonna sit here all day or what?" I made a quick calculation noting that the fire department was less than three blocks away, just in case this "Witch" caught fire walking into a Church of Christian faith.

We got out and made our way to the doors of my new "Faith and Home".

Chapter Eight
"Becoming a Family of Faith"

I walked into our local church named *Faith Family*, and I was immediately taken. The motto was "Better Fathers, Better Mothers, Stronger Families." I had found my HOME Church because let's face it I have failed on each of these daily.

I remember Myke texting me when he woke up, it was just as we were getting ready to sit down for service. "Where are you at?" To which I replied, "Went to Church". His response to that was "Yeah right, where are you?" I ended up sending him a picture of the back of someone's seat to show him I was really sitting in a church and that it wasn't actually on fire or imploding.

I remember the sermon that day, it was on the wide path and narrow road. The scripture was:

> ***Matthew 7: 13-14, "Enter through the narrow gate. For wide is the gate and broad is the road that leads to destruction, and many enter through it. But small is the gate and narrow the road that leads to life, and only a few find it."***

As I sat there in Awe, wondering if someone had called ahead to the Pastor and told him "You have a crazy Wicca Witch lady coming that lost a child. She is lost and broken, have the fire extinguisher ready." Because as I sat there and listened to him, it was as if he was speaking directly to my soul, coring me of my existence and filling me with Jesus Christ. It was an Ahh Ha moment for me. I literally felt him speaking to my soul. During this service I remember him getting choked up while telling a personal story. He was speaking to me in ways that I never knew were possible. I looked around at people leaning in and listening to him. I left there that day knowing a few things:

1. My world needed to change in a right now, do not look back kind of way.
2. I have always taken the easy wide roadway in life, and so far, that was really sucking for me.
3. I was a complete failure at the foundation of our family.
4. I wanted more, I wanted to be fed, and
5. I needed God to do what he could only do. FIX ME.

I began attending church weekly in 2016, so did our younger children. They enjoyed it; I began to see changes both in their behaviors and in my family.

We made big changes in our home. We began being Christ centered. I slowly began finding my voice again. I began to read and try to understand the bible. I started to find scripture that could directly tell me I was going to hell if I continued down the prior dark path again.

Because I still was tempted all the time with the "Dark Side". I remember one morning waking up and my young son's brown leather bible that had a tree on the cover was sitting on the kitchen table. Pastor Rob gifted him this bible at camp, he carried it everywhere. It was sitting on my kitchen table and was open to Micah. There was a napkin laying on the page and it was underlining *Micah 5:12,*

> *"I will destroy your witchcraft*
> *and you will no longer*
> *cast spells."*

To this day I have no idea how that happened. I had not been reading the bible, in fact it was not even in that same room. Our younger children were with my husband at camp. He was giving me a break to get a few needed things done in the house. This is still a complete mystery to me, or God's divine intervention perhaps? But when something so blatantly comes and slaps you in the face you obey. I sat at our kitchen table and read that verse multiple times. I was still wondering how this bible was there, opened to Micah, with a napkin underling the very verse I needed to see, read, and then read again.

I then decided to go farther and search for more. I opened my phone and searched the words "bible scripture on witchcraft and evil" making note of a few, I was shocked to see there were near 100 biblical scriptures regarding Witchcraft. It hit me like a ton of bricks as I sat there reading some of the scripture in my son's little brown bible with the imprinted tree on the front telling me everything I wish I would have known when I was 16 years old.

That day it ended. I took my small black hard-cover book that contained almost 20 years of Wicca writings, spells, rituals, effects and my personal journal of my practices along with everything that had anything to do with the "dark side", walked outside, put it in the small fireplace burn pit we had in the corner of our yard and burned it all. I sat there and watched what was taking place in that small burn pit. I watched almost 20 years of my life burn and I did not have one uneasy feeling or concern about this. In fact, it gave me a feeling of calmness, freedom, positivity, and for the first time in a long-time. Complete peace.

To this day I do not know if my husband knew I did this. I am quite sure he had no clue at all about any of it because he has never mentioned a word about it. But I do believe that I did the right thing and I have never looked back.

The more that I surrendered myself to Jesus, the more my family life began to fall into place. The more that I began understanding the words in the bible, the more I healed. The difference became words jumping off the pages at me verses not understanding a word that I was reading prior to that day.

I remember when I began missing Jacob for the first time, instead of being angry each time I thought of him. That feeling was amazing. I was sitting in the kitchen making Jacob's favorite homemade mac and cheese, because my son Charles requested it. This was when for the first time I ACTUALLY MISSED HIM. I was not mad. But standing there cutting the block of cheese by hand, made me smile in memory. To this day whenever a child requests "Grandma May's homemade mac and cheese" I still do the same, each cut, and each layer I make. I can now smile my way thru it remembering Jacob.

What an epiphany! Why did I not do this sooner? I then began to feel the sorrow and grief. I am not going to lie, this made me angry as hell. I was angry because I thought what I had been going thru since Jake died was grief. It was actually destruction of myself due to not having faith. So, lucky me, I got to relive this twice in two different ways.

It was not until Jesus Christ completely wiped me clean and rebuilt me that I was able to process the thought of Grief and missing my child. Let me say this again. **IT WASN'T UNTIL I SURRENDERED, SURRENDERED IT ALL TO JESUS CHRIST AND LET HIM REBUILD ME, LEVEL ME, AND HEAL ME THAT I BEGAN TO ACTUALLY LIVE AGAIN.**

I completely surrendered my life and accepted my Savior Jesus Christ on September 18th, 2018. I was baptized at our local campground by the pastor of my church Pastor Paul. This day I was surrounded by my husband, younger children, and my mother along with many from our church. I remember looking up at my mother as she had tears in her eyes. She had found her own faith as well making this an answered prayer. As Pastor Paul had me stand in front of everyone and share a brief testimony of my surrendering, he helped cover my face as he immersed me in the water and brought me back to the surface pure and born again. I was wearing a long white dress this day. I had to smile that this was the very spot that Jacob years prior swam with his brothers and saved us all from the snake.

I was Redeemed and Forgiven, but I was also a survivor and I had a fire in my soul. I began reading the bible, my own this time. The words began jumping off the page at me. I had been going to church faithfully for about a year prior to my being baptized, and I was still learning, but one thing I knew was this: I could not and would not go back to my dark ways.

I still have constant reminders of my darker days. Today's social media has no grace in that. It is still hard for me that social media memories pop up about Jacob. I am so lucky that I get to relive these moments every time one pops up. I say this lightly because I realize how sick I really was at that time I clicked share now.

I wished harm to the boy who killed my son, I shared hate. I had no grace. Jacob was such a gentle soul; he would not hurt anyone; he was forgiving and resilient. This is such a moment of accountability to me, in a sick kind of way. Today I have empathy for who killed my son, I have empathy and grief for his mother who lost her son as well. Today I can forgive him for killing my son, because my God has already paid that price.

I still share those memories; although they are set to private so that only I can see them. Lord Jesus, if they ever accidently shared publicly, I would have some of my "Jesus Sisters" blowing my phone up. I would never share that with anyone again. This way, each year I have that accountability of what NOT to do.

I know that I have so much farther to go in my relationship with Christ. But I know I can do all things thru him because he truly does strengthen me. But I cannot ever lose my faith again because he is not done with me yet.

Once I saw what Christ can do in my "broken" home, it became a non-negotiable rule in the home. I had already screwed up with my now adult children, by not making this a priority. I failed them in this, just as my parents unintentionally failed me.

I continued to go and get involved with our church. The more involved I became the more that I noticed my younger children asking to partake. It was a fantastic transition in every way, shape, and form. My children began asking every Saturday, "Do we get to go to church tomorrow?" They enjoyed it and looked forward to it. We became a family of faith.

> **Hebrews 10:25, "Not giving up meeting together, as some are in the habit of doing, but encouraging one another – and all the more as you see the Day approaching."**

The Bible says to make a habit of going to church. Most of the time when we think of habits, we think of bad but there is good. Going to church sets a positive example. For those of you who are married, it is a positive example to your spouse. For those of you that have children, it is a positive example for your kids to know that on Sunday you go to church. For the people around you when they see that you have a commitment that is leading you to living a better life, that is a positive example that other people can follow.

It is a wonderful thing to be a part of a local church. It is like having a much larger family. The service you miss is the service you need.

Chapter Nine
"The Face of Death"

Let us begin this chapter first by thinking about death. I think this chapter could be placed earlier in this book. But leading into the next chapter, I felt that it needed to be placed here to properly lead up to what is about to take place. When thinking about death understand that we will not stop there. Death is really a celebration of life and its memories, a celebration of our faith and hope. Which is rooted in the resurrection of Jesus.

Important events of our lives, like a memorial service or a funeral, are communal and somewhat ritualized. Meaning, no matter where we come, we know what to expect at a memorial service: sitting in silence, family processional, scripture, hymns, reflections, food, and mourning. Memorials and Funerals are not for our loved ones who have passed, they are really for those left behind. Our loved ones who have passed on have already entered their eternal life, we are still in our temporary home.

Nobody likes to talk about death, yet that word is mentioned over 400 times in the bible.

The face of Death can seem like the end, you often lower a casket into the ground to cover your loved one up or you are handed a special box with their remains and you never get to hear their voice again. You feel as if there is no hope. That life will never go back to the way it was. You just feel empty, like it is done. So we are supposed to just grin, move on, and bear it.

But yet, we come to the understanding that in Christ there is NO death.

~He has defeated death

~He is the hope

~He is the way

~He is new life

Christ brings forth new life. He does this, during and even after life. With this earthly death of emptiness and hopelessness becomes a spiritual rebirth of:

~A new body

~A new world

~A new beautiful kingdom

This is called Eternity in Heaven. In Christ, our face of death can become a beautiful anticipation of a grand party. A reunion like no other. Like a bride waiting for her groom, as she awaits a beautiful ceremony, and a courtship of families becoming one with no separation ever to be again. The face of death no longer carries that sting of the end, but the antidote for your broken heart to carry on with Jesus's eternal love and promise to carry you to the very beginning, not just a ritual celebrating your earthly remains.

Death is a persistent reminder that life is a paradox and a puzzle. We are born, dependent on care and nurturing from our parents; we mature and accomplish life's tasks as best we can; we believe and we doubt, we struggle and we conquer, and, eventually, some grow older, we become more and more dependent, and it is inevitable we all die. Expressed so well in Psalms 39: 4-9,

> *4Show me, LORD, my life's end and the number of my days; let me know how fleeting my life is. 5You have made my days a mere handbreadth; the span of my years is as nothing before you. Everyone is but a breath, even those who seem secure. 6Surely everyone goes around like a mere phantom; in vain they rush about, heaping up wealth without knowing whose it will finally be. 7But now, LORD, what do I look for? My hope is in you. 8Save me from all my transgressions; do not make me the scorn of fools. 9I was silent; I would not open my mouth, for you are the one who has done this.*

There are no exceptions. But death, even though it comes to all, is not always the same. It comes with many different faces.

Death is God's way of bringing life on earth to a fitting conclusion. When he calls us home, our life here on earth is completed. Earth is not our permanent dwelling place it really is just temporary.

Our loved ones are only loaned to us here on earth, once we are called home to our eternity, everything on earth that takes place is just for the family and loved ones left behind. Although death is painful for those of us who are left.

I had a long conversation with a friend named Jacquie. I'm thankful she is always willing to help me process my thoughts prior to any speaking engagement. While I was preparing to officiate my nephew's memorial service, she said, "No one is getting out of here alive. This life is but an intermission, of the big show. You better get your ticket, that price for it has been paid!" This is the true meaning of everlasting love. **MIC DROP MOMENT:**

"TEAR MY TICKET FOR ADMISSION."

Remember, our sorrow and grief are tempered with gratitude and many memories of shared experiences – gratitude that the struggle is over, and memories that we will cherish long after God calls our loved one home. Although we grieve, we can also live. Live in the moment of the good, do not just focus on the "gone aspect", instead focus on the "HOME" aspect. Just that minor thought process change really does make a HUGE difference in your perception.

Chapter Ten
"My Lil'Man"

Please give me grace while doing Jarred's story, because to keep it true to Jarred, I need to represent him in a way that may jump around a bit. Jarred was unique in his own right. He has a powerful story. But for me to tell it properly it must be told in a way that might seem to jump around for the reader. Understand, I did not find my faith until Jarred was almost 17 years old. So, when reading this portion, read it from the standpoint that his original foundation was that of "nonfaith," it was not until he was 17 that he began to believe.

Jarred's story is one that is quite different, a survivor story of sorts. Which is a very ironic part in his personal story.

Jarred was born in October of 1999. He was a pleasant surprise. He entered the world raising hell and honestly never stopped. Jarred was most definitely what one would call a "mommas boy". The youngest of 4 boys at the time, he literally was strapped to my body in either a backpack or wrap until the age of almost two.

Looking back at this, I really wish I would have cherished those small things a bit more. Like I said earlier, I really thought I knew what I was doing, and I failed at multiple levels in their lives. I think every parent of grown children looking back says the same thing.

The biggest failure being that I did not raise them to have faith. Jarred had a rough and turbulent life. He was diagnosed ADHD by age 6 and we fell into the medication roulette game by age 7. He began having severe adverse reactions to the medications he was on. One in particular causing severe night terrors. The type of night terrors where he would wake my husband up in the middle of the night, walk with him into a different room then begin "fighting air". We would often wake up and he would be sleeping in his drawer, another room once even the bathtub. On one occasion my husband went out to warm his car up in the early morning for work. While scraping the snow off the windows, he noticed little bare footprints in the snow walking around our lake house. Jarred had a night terror and went outside of our house in the middle of the night in the snow. That day my husband installed alarms and special locks on all our doors so that we would be alerted to this if he opened the door. Watching Jarred sleep at that time was most definitely an "action film in motion".

My mother called me one day while I was at work saying, "You have to see this." Knowing the issues, we were having with him. She then sent me a news article on the medication he was on. I immediately hung up and called his pediatrician. While I was on hold waiting for the front desk to transfer me to Pam, Jarred's favorite nurse. The Doctor was calling me on my work phone at the same time. I hung up from my cell phone and accepted the call and, low and behold, she had just seen the documentation on it as well. We IMMEDIATELY began the 6-month process weaning him from that medicine. Yes, it took 6 months to wean him off a medication that he took once daily. He never had another night terror again after that.

It took us years to figure this out. We could not figure out what was going on, he had been to sleep doctors, sleep studies, multiple different doctors, therapists and Psychologists. He was just labeled a difficult child in every sense of the meaning of the word difficult. Each professional had the same answer, "Let's try this medication." By the time my son was 8 he was on 4 different medications.

Little did we know he was struggling with Mental Illness. Jarred was diagnosed as Bipolar Mania Type Depression Disorder at age 12, we had been medicating him wrong all along. Talk about a slap in your face as a parent. We had been giving him ADHD medications that were counteracting with his mental health diagnosis. With my grandmother's mental health history we really should have known this. She loved waking me up as a child with tea parties and Jarred loved waking us up as a child to fight an action film.

He was not ADHD; it was much worse. Once we had him accurately diagnosed, his life went smoother until I fell off the face of the living earth when Jacob died. We had just gotten Jarred and his mental health figured out when Jacob was murdered.

Thru my destruction process when Jacob died, I lost a part of my son Jarred that I never quite got back. I did not even realize it until it was too late. Talk about another level of grief, this self-caused. I gave my family a 3 for 1 deal.

Again, Jarred made choices of his own free will, some good, some terrible and some that were literally life altering. At the age of 12 he began his own path of destruction.

He was "jumped" into his first gang at age 13, by 14 he was running weapons for a gang in the city, by 15 he was dabbling in drugs, and by 16 he was heading to prison.

One day from jail he wrote me a letter asking me to pray for him because I had told him that the devil got his soul. This hit me hard after losing Jake. I was thinking to myself, "I have danced with the devil literally," what if he died like Jake?" Where would his eternity be?

He was on formal court probation by the age of 14 and expelled from school. Mrs. Birchmeier, the principle who always protected my boys, was now the assistant principle at the school he was attending and was about to expel him for putting her school at risk. She was with him this day as well and although the choice he made in school that day was severe, she never left his side. How ironic was it that the very lady who protected my children during the media frenzy was now protecting the school from my son? I remember walking into the office that day and looking at her face. I was frantic, because the principle had called me and only said "I need you to get to the school right away, it is urgent regarding your son Jarred." I left my grocery cart where it was and drove to school in a panicked hurry. I pulled into the school noticing that there were police cars in the driveway. I immediately thought he was dead, because let's face it, given his history that seemed plausible.

Mrs. Birchmeier saw my face when I walked in. She was leaning against her office door waiting for me. We made direct eye contact and I believe she knew what I was thinking, I could see it in her face. She put both of her hands up and said these words to me in a firm raised voice "ANG STOP HE IS OKAY, he is right here." I rushed past her to see his face. I was happy he was okay, but once she told me that he decided to bring a loaded weapon to school he was incredibly lucky to be alive. In fact, I may have wanted to kill him myself for a moment or ten if I am being completely honest. If you are a parent of a teen with mental health issues I am sure you have been there at least once or a hundred times.

Thru all this Jarred had a fantastic support system behind him always thru his delinquency, we were very blessed to have Probation Officer Scott and our local Judges, both in Probate and then District. He really was blessed with people who genuinely cared for him. He was doing okay on probation, but he had some slip ups, so his probation officer suggested boot camp.

We put him in a local boot camp that he thrived in, even graduating honor company. Jarred really did well unless he was in active Mania. Which sadly happened about every 6-8 months. At that time, it generally ended with front page news of some sort.

We finally found a therapist that "got him", he loved her. For the first time after 6 different therapist, 4 different Psychologists and a mile-long list of testing, we finally found one he worked well with and just understood him. Cathy was her name, and she is still is a special part of our lives.

Some days she had to chase him down for a session, quite literally chase him down. She never gave up on him, in fact in a few sessions she would walk out with him, red faced and just shaking her head. I remember once, she and he had a tense appointment where Jarred was being very candid with her about some of his "gang related activity". She walked out with him, looked at me with a tear in her eye, she couldn't even formulate a "goodbye" or anything, she simply said, "I will text you." We left, and I got a text that said, "Thursday at 1:00 pm." I highly suspect she may have attended her own therapy session directly after that one. Jarred and Cathy had a special relationship, when I say she got him she really did. He used to always tell her, "When I make it big I'm going to buy you a pink diamond like that one from the Titanic." She ultimately got that very thing. It currently hangs on her mirror in her home with his cremated remains in it.

Around this time in 2017, he began dating a young lady named Shiann who had a daughter that was about 8 months old at the time. Their story was interesting in the fact that her daughter now became Jarred's daughter and our granddaughter. Their relationship did not make it for the long haul, but their friendship always remained.

That little girl gave him a new meaning in life, he knew what it was like to love someone so much that you wanted to be a better person. This little girl is 4 today and still a HUGE part of our lives. We call her by her nickname "Sassy". She was not from his flesh, but she sure was from his heart.

His little girl has a love for Jesus, her Pastor, and going to church. Jarred would be super proud of how smart she is. We are blessed with the fact that her Mother and her maternal family allow us to still see her, support her and of course bring her up in faith. There are days when she opens her mouth, and her daddy comes out. It is sometimes a fantastic reminder and other times "Did she really just say that?"

Crazy enough thru all the negative behaviors that Jarred had, he NEVER brought that crazy to our home or hers. He in fact always protected his family from this. He was protective to a fault over his family.

No matter what he did outside of our home, he never actually brought it home. In this I could always see the light in his darkness, even as the prison walls began to set in as a possibility for him. Jarred went to jail for the first time at the age of 17, he was in an active Mania and thought it would be a great idea to resist a police officer, or more like FIVE of them.

I knew the road he was heading down. I personally went to our Judge and told him to keep him in jail so we could get him back on his medications and get his Mania under control. You read that right, I asked him to keep my child incarcerated.

I literally walked into the Judge's chambers, knocked on the half door he had and his aide let me into speak to him. I explained what had been taking place and what we were doing to try to help. I begged him, "KEEP HIM IN JAIL," or offer a high bond so that his idiot friends he was running with at that time could not bail him out, I needed time. Oh my gosh, I had become my actual mother in a nutshell. This is the very thing she use to do when my brothers got into trouble. I look back at this now and laugh. Because If I am ½ of who my mother is, I will take that.

The Judge must have thought I was nuts, in fact he said this was a first for him. I am still thankful today for this Judge in our local District court.

I remember the day at his arraignment. I was sitting in the front row when my son was brought into the court room, he looked over at me and mouthed, "I love you mom, I'm sorry." For a second I felt bad knowing what was about to happen to him, maybe about a half second.

As I sat there in the front row, staring at the view from behind of my son, he was dressed in a ridiculously large jumpsuit, labeled with the County Jail, orange flip flops that were way too big for him and his hands were cuffed behind his back. I can still hear the chains around his ankles rattling and shaking as he walked by. The Judge looked around his shoulder at me, took his glasses off and looked at Jarred.

Jarred immediately knew, in fact he looked at the ground and began shaking his head. He knew what I had done.

The judge looked at him and said, "Young man, I could give you a Personal Recognizance bond but (he looked at me from the bench) Jarred immediately turned his head to follow where he was looking, and he shook his head and mouthed to me "You didn't", I grinned of course. The judge went on and stated, "I'm going to hold you so your mom can get a good night's sleep and work some things out for you, 20,000.00 Cash Surety bond is ordered."

Jarred, as he was walking out of the courtroom, handcuffed behind his back looked at me and gave me his legendary smirk, and just shook his head. As I left court that day the Judge said, "MOM", I stopped and turned and he goes, "We need more mothers like you, you may have just saved your son's life." I had to do something. I was losing another child. We made the necessary arrangements to get the proper medications to the jail, he took them without any issue. He knew he needed to get his "levels" back up. His attorney at the time had a new bond hearing for him, we asked for release with some stipulations, which were granted.

He got out of jail and was doing fantastic, in fact making great changes. He began mentoring at risk children and going to church some with me. He was grasping some faith; he began preaching to kids his age about his past and where it had led him. There were still issues from time to time if his level's fell. Once requiring inpatient residential for 5 days to help. But all and all if he took his medication, he did okay.

Jarred attended a church service one day and I remember this day so well. I made him dress appropriately for church, meaning no what I called "ghetto thug like clothing". He loved pants with holes in them, graphic t-shirts that were not always appropriate and hoodies along with his signature beanie hat he wore. I never understood his appeal to those pants, he would pay $100 for them, when I offered to go to the thrift store and put holes in them myself for $3.00.

This day he got up, showered, put on a pair of his white knit shorts and a white T shirt along with his tennis shoes and socks. I remember him walking out of the bathroom and saying, "Is this good enough for church?" I simply replied, "It will do."

We got to church and sat down. The service that day was on "breaking chains of bondage". Jarred got called upon the stage by our Pastor who began placing himself in a strait jacket. Again, my Pastor just knows who needs to be cored I suspect. Because he did it again, but this time to my troubled son.

As I sat there watching my son on stage, helping my Pastor, padlock, and latch, buckle and wrap chains around his white strait jacket it occurred to me what was taking place. Jarred was surrendering his life right before my eyes. He in his own way was breaking his own chains and was handing it all over to Christ. We left church that day, and while heading to an event, a popular Christian song came on the radio about breaking chains.

Jarred began singing this song on repeat and even rapping it. I was in AWE. From that day forward Jarred tried to stay on the narrow path, he failed often as the wheel of mental health goes but the intent to do better was always there.

He began changing his life, leaving negative groups, and kicking his addiction. I could not have been prouder. During this time Jarred also began an outreach out of our home, where he gave free clothing to homeless, foster families and any one of need. We now call this "Jarred's Bow-Tie closet".

Jarred was so much more than just a troubled kid. Although he did have his share of battles, there was so much more to him. He was one who wanted to preach his story to others in hopes of helping them remain on the right path. He was able to do this in a way that really hit the core of those that were just like him. Often times, I sat in admiration watching him speak to youth. He would always begin every time with "I'm just gonna preach." The people he was speaking to just sat down, and tuned in to his commanded attention. He knew both the right and the wrong way to do things. Let's face it, he learned that the hard way.

I remember one time in particular hearing Jarred speak to youth's that have had a turbulent life like he did. He was at Honor Company at the boot camp he attended, I arrived to pick him up and as I walked into the gym area where they were at, I noticed him off to the side speaking to a young man not much younger than him.

I sat there and just listened to him speak to this youth about the "Jonah and the Whale" story in the bible. I can hear his voice in my head still today and see his hand motions as he spoke about Jonah being swallowed by this big fish. It still makes me smile when I think of this. He was telling this youth that Jonah tried to run away from God. He got to the end of his story and simply looked at this youth and said, "So are you ready to be puked up and make things right yet." I had to laugh at this point, because this was most definitely a true method of delivery for Jarred.

Jonah 2:1-10, "From inside the fish Jonah prayed to the LORD his God. He said: 'In my distress I called to the LORD, and he answered me. From deep in the realm of the dead I called for help, and you listened to my cry. You hurled me into the depths, into the very heart of the seas, and the currents swirled about me; all your waves and breakers swept over me. I said, 'I have been banished from your sight; yet I will look again toward your holy temple. The engulfing waters threatened me, the deep surrounded me; seaweed was wrapped around my head. To the roots of the mountains I sank down; the earth beneath barred me in forever. But you, LORD my God, brought my life up from the pit.' 'When my life was ebbing away, I remembered you, LORD, and my prayer rose to you, to your holy temple. Those who cling to worthless idols turn away from God's love for them. But I, with shouts of grateful praise, will sacrifice to you. What I have vowed I will make good. I will say, Salvation comes from the LORD.' And the LORD commanded the fish, and it vomited Jonah onto dry land."

Here is the thing. When we as parents have a troubled child, other parents question the experiences of joy and being proud over small things. I have been asked "Why are you proud for something that should have been done all along?" Well because it is all in God's timing not yours. I appreciated the small steps my child was making in his life. I remember the judgment other parents made about Jarred. It broke me, they only knew the headlines, they had no idea of the son, brother, nephew, grandchild, or cousin that he was.

It was hard living in that glass house of judgement. People sometimes were ruthless. My parenting was attacked by many. People did not understand sometimes that I have other children who were successful and thriving. Most had no idea of the mental health issues Jarred had. I did not completely understand it myself. I know how I felt so I can only imagine how many questions, feelings, and thoughts that my own son had regarding his mental health.

One summer I was introduced to a book called *Breaking Bipolar* by Troy Steven, this book helped me understand the cycles that my son had gone thru. I only wish I had read this book sooner. In a way this book let me own my own feelings that I was not crazy along with my son. Troy said it best when he stated, "Living with Bipolar Disorder is truly a war." It certainly was, it was a war for both my son and his family.

One thing I knew was that Jarred was better than he was the previous day. He was really trying and doing well. In fact, many would say he was doing the best he had ever done. He was attending church on occasion and staying out of trouble. The more I witnessed him helping others, the more I noticed that it was helping him as well. We were finally on a narrow path and in a good routine. I had hope in his future, little did I know that the future we had planned would be vastly different than what was about to take place.

Ecclesiastes 3:11, "He has made everything beautiful in its time. He has also set eternity in the human heart; yet no one can fathom what God has done from beginning to end."

Chapter Eleven
"I just Wanna Preach by Jarred"

It still was not easy, but I had peace knowing he was working toward being a better person. I am going to get candid and share some of his "I'm just gonna preach moments" written by him directly.

This is hard for me to do because these were his personal words, he wrote and left. I will warn you now he did have some colorful language that I will not redact because I want it to remain true to his actual words, I guess what teens call "hip lingo". I call it "Non-English ghetto slang." So, understand the wording is his, I was told it is how teens speak today. I will only redact names to protect anonymity. But this is what prepared me for what would take place next, in Jarred's life. The Do-Over. The blessings that these left me with are vast, even with some of them repeating some of the same things. I believe it was his own testimony that he continued to write.

Jarred Burns 06/16/2017 (Writing he did in Jail, I found in his drawer after he passed away).

My momma prays for me every night, I sat in that cell thinking I'm going straight to hell. I remember sitting in jail on the phone and my momma goes "boy the devil got ahold of you" and I said yeah I know just pray for me I'll pray I get some hope, I know I got it right because when I was 15 I was looking at hard time in juvie and God took care of me!

I have always thought respect was being the baddest dude or strongest person, so I always tried to get respect in that way. But now I see it is a lot more than that. Now I want to be remembered for the good reasons like helping people and doing good things. I want to be respected for the right reasons. The person that gives the shirt off their back to somebody in need the person that sends food to people who are hungry. The person that will do anything for anybody when they ain't finna do it for themselves.

Man, I make my momma crazy when I do this. She always thinking I am in (TOWN) when that alert comes thru! Man I learned a lot, about my friends and some of my so-called friends someone told me no more negative people and it clicked negative people equal negative outcomes. I'm finna drop and forget the negative people in my life. I'm gonna move away to do this. This town is bad for me I ain't staying clean here.

I wanna be respected for good reasons like helping someone or doing good. I don't want to be respected for being able to beat someone up like that's not respect that's fear, and I ain't gonna be that person anymore, the hardest thing happened to me when I was in jail. That was seeing my little brother through a glass window it was hard as hell for both of us and I'm his big brother he looks up to me and don't want that ever to happen again.

I want to keep helping kids like me. Kids that have the same problems as me. People used to count on me to have guns drugs and other things they needed.

If you're reading this right now think what it's like having those kind of people count on you to make those things happen. Have you ever had people's lives on the line?

Everyone says oh Jarred that kid that got expelled from school oh Jarred that kid that likes to fight oh Jarred that kid that likes to beat people up oh Jarred that kid that got in a fight with a cop no man **I'm just Jarred just a normal kid just troubled.**

6/19/2017 Writing from Jail

I've always thought respect was being the baddest dude or strongest person so I always tried to get respect in that way. But now I wanna be re-spected for the good reasons like helping people and just good reasons,

I wanna be respected for the right reasons. Some-one wrote me and it was someone I care about a lot and she said "no more negative people, so I thought you're a negative person and your telling me no more negative people so I wrote her back and told her we cant be friends no more because no more negative people. My Autumn already been saying this to me. It didn't make sense to me then but it does now. Negative people equal negative out-comes.

July 2017 Writing from Jail

Since I have been in Jail I've realized a lot, about me and my friends. Or so-called friends. Someone said no more negative people and it clicked, nega-tive people equal negative outcome, so when I get out im prepared to drop and forget the negative people in my life.

I also wanna be respected for good reasons like helping someone or doing good. I don't wanna be respected for being able to beat someone up that's not respect that's fear and I don't wanna be that person, seeing my little brother threw a glass win-dow it was hard on both of us and I'm his big brother he looks up to me. When I get out I'm going to become someone he can really look up to for good reasons.

My goals when I get out are to finish school and start working at boot camp where they want me to come help kids that have had the same problems as me.

Then at some point I would like to go to college and get a job. I have been clean from drugs for a year and I'm ready to get out of here and become the person people will look up to. I am going to move to my grandmas where Imma go to school and help my grandma and go to church.

July, 2017 Writing to his Step Mother Teresa, he actually colored her a picture of a lion and on the back he wrote:

Bad things happen before good things happen.

August 29th, 2017

"I just wanna preach" social media post

"I just wanna preach, if you die as u are rn would you be fully satisfied with your life? Answer this not to me but in your head, would I be happy? Yes I have had a great life and God needs me for a reason. I may be a shitty kid but God loves all? Murders, junkies, people that steal, God loves all. No person can be so bad for the love of our God. So better yourself not for God because he accepts you for you, but better yourself for your family and yourself."

Imma just preach (social media) 12/23/17

I went to church tonight with my momma, I am on the right track. Let me ask "In light of eternity does what your doing matter" change is hard. But knowing my eternity now is worth change. I got approached by someone at church who made things right with me, man he come walking toward me and I was like bro don't make me do this in front of my momma. Not here! He crouched down and made it right, I expected the worse I have been where he was and I have done the same thing. Bigger man to man up and make it right than walk away. Same service I was being threatened by text by someone, hell he threatened my momma too. She looked at me and said "don't! you know who you are now" she right I walked away, I ain't finna be that person no more. My eternity straight!"

That evening Jarred was attending our candle-light service for Christmas Eve. He helped serve communion to the congregation with a mutual friend. This day Jarred took his first communion ever.

He left church and headed home with his buddy and I texted him and told him I loved him and was proud of him and he responded with this text:

"It's just hard not doing what I use to."

Little did I know he would enter his eternity on 12/25/2017.

In Jarred's own words "Bad things happen before good things happen." We know this statement all too well. With Jarred there was a lot of bad, but there was even more amounts of good in his story.

When you have a rough and turbulent life as he did, we celebrated each positive that we got to see. To me each one of these "I just wanna preach" that he left us, gives me hope and peace that he understood the seeds that I planted in him later in his life. It only takes a mustard seed remember. I just wish I had planted this seed in Jarred earlier in his life. I have hope that it was, some of the letters and notes he wrote my mother much younger in his life attest to this. But it certainly was not planted by me until he was almost 17 years old.

I know today that his words continue to help and mentor kids that have gone through the same trials and tribulations that he did. In fact, during his memorial our Pastor used his **"Im just Jarred just a normal kid just troubled."** It became a hashtag on social media because it really did sum up my son in one short sentence. One of his siblings even got this very line permanently inked on her skin. He was just a normal kid, he just struggled with some trouble but he didn't let that define him.

It still amazes me today when I get a request from someone that asks me to repost a certain "I just wanna preach" or a certain video that Jarred had previously written or recorded. I know that Jarred's testimony although delivered in a different way than most, is a powerful rendition of his faith.

I can only come to one conclusion. Salvation is a gift from God, but if your life does not show evidence of God working in it, then you likely never received the **Gift of Deliverance**. The reality is God uses Trials and Tribulations to improve and strengthen our faith in him. The godly reason for trials in our lives is faith related. It is a faith-based issue. Trials and Tribulations test, prove and build our faith and represent the likeness of Christ in us.

With trials and tribulations it is easy to become frustrated with the circumstance we find ourselves in. We can often feel like God is against us or not interested, or we can change our perspective, and advance our lives by gaining the Spiritual maturity we might be needing. This could be counted as a blessing if looked at thru a different lens. The goal of trials is not to make us more preserving. Rather it is just the road traveled to get to the goal. That is very motivating to me.

God has assured us that He will not permit us to be attacked with trials or tribulations that are too devastating for us to handle. He will grant us grace to conquer. As God faithfully pours out His grace upon us during each circumstance, we can survive hardships and overcome the enemy in God's strength. This is written about so many times in the bible.

> *Romans 5:3-5, "Not only so, but we also glory in our sufferings, because we know that suffering produces perseverance; perseverance, character; and character, hope. And hope does not put us to shame, because God's love has been poured out into our hearts through the Holy Spirit, who has been given to us."*

> *James: 1:12, "Blessed is the one who perseveres under trial because, having stood the test, that person will receive the crown of life that the lord has promised to those who love him."*

> *Joshua 1:9, "Have I not commanded you? Be strong and courageous. Do not be afraid; do not be discouraged, for the Lord your God will be with you wherever you go."*

Chapter Three: "The Do-Over" "Jarred" (Yes, I know we are on Chapter Three again)

We had Christmas 2017 at my Mom's that year; we were there as a family. We did the traditional things, opened gifts, ate a traditional supper, and spent time together. Jarred's friend was picking him back up about 8:30 pm. I made all my kids stand not knowing that would be the last picture that we took of Jarred. I remember Charles griping about having to take a picture. Like he always did, because he hates pictures.

I even said "Hey, what if it is the last one?" as I put my kids in line, the adult children in back and the younger children in front, and snapped the button on my phone.

I remember thinking to myself something was not right. But with Jarred, it was different, because with him you just never knew, there was always something not right, but you picked your battles. He was standing, alive, not in handcuffs and was present. Mother's that have dealt with children in trouble will understand that mother's instinct and also the dismissal that something was not right. I took a few more pictures with my phone and we all said our goodbyes.

I hugged Jarred tight and whispered in his ear. "Be careful son, I love you." He replied back "I love you too, don't worry about me I'll be fine," as he walked out the door. That rang in my head because Jarred did not even know that is almost verbatim what Jacob said to me the last time I spoke to him.

I still have issues today with people who do not say "Bye", it triggers me in a way that is still not quite healthy. I am talking if I am speaking to someone on the phone and they hang up without saying goodbye. I will call them back to find out if their phone is broken, if they died, or if they just hung up on me.

We left my mom's that night and headed home exhausted. I had texted Jarred a "goodnight" about 10:10 pm. I did not get a text back, but this was not weird because his phone battery was always dead, or he would often respond much later. Me, being a snarky mom I sent a second text, "If you don't start responding to my texts, I'm going to think you're dead or I may just shut your phone off." I got nothing back, again which was not abnormal, he would respond later, and I would wake up to the text, or so I thought. So, my husband and I crawled into bed exhausted and fell asleep. I remember praying that night to "God" thanking him for such a great day at my mom's house and the opportunity to see my kids all together. I asked him to keep them all safe and for his will to be done.

I was awakened by my phone in the early hours of the morning to one word, the one word that had haunted me in my sleep since 2012. The very word I heard in early April, 2012. I looked at the caller ID, knowing he did not have any of the boys this time, I knew something was bad. He had no reason to call me that early. I got out of bed already in a panic, pacing in our bedroom. I answered this time "Hello" and I heard it. I heard the very word that rocked my world in 2012. "AAANNNNGGGGG," even more strangled than the last time.

I dropped to the floor because by process of elimination I knew it was Jarred. Alexys and Charles came back here to stay with their younger siblings after leaving my moms, Gavin was at his house and Robert at his home with his wife and two sons. I KNEW it was Jarred. I began screaming "NO NO NO!" My husband woke up in a panic wondering what was wrong. Jarred's dad went on and said "O my God, not again. AAANNNNGGG I don't even know how to say this, I can't even say it, Jarred is dead, it was an accident but he is dead." I dropped to the ground. I did not say a word, he went on, "He was shot, it was an accident, he shot himself in the head, but they said it was an accident. " I do not remember what I said next. Everything came back to me; it was a blur. I sent Myke downstairs to wake up the older kids and gave him a verbal list of calls to make. I remember saying to him specifically, as he was walking out of the door and heading downstairs. "Do not call my mom I will call her. Do not call my mom, she has to hear this from me."

He walked out of the room, phone in hand, in shock I am sure. I dropped to my knees sobbing and I prayed,

> *"God, I can't do this again without you, please surround me with your peace and show me what I need to do this time, this is going to be hard for everyone, he was a huge part of people's lives. Do not let me screw up this time. Help me to not go down that wide path again, keep me on your narrow road, God help me get thru this knowing he is now home with you. Amen."*

I still remember that prayer like it was yesterday. I picked up the phone and called my mom and she answered on the first ring, I swear she never sleeps. I said, "Hello Mom," she replied, "What happened, is it Jarred?" I replied simply, "I need you to come now." She replied, "Ok, I'm on my way." She didn't even say "Bye", she just hung up.

After we hung up I sat on my bed for a few moments before going downstairs. I remember looking up and saying out loud "**No, I can't do this again, GOD I CANNOT do this again.**" It was clear as day, I heard it, I literally heard the Holy Spirit speak to me,

> *"Do good, do good deeds, reach people, help people, turn every hurt into grace and good, stay in the light, use his story and help as many people as he would have."*

This began my new face of Grief. My "Do Over". It still hurts me today to say that, because man I would not wish that pain on anyone EVER. I heard a "strangled scream" of sorts from downstairs, I knew my husband had just told our daughter Alexys, who was Jarred's best friend as well. They were extremely close. They had an incredibly unique and devoted relationship. They were not just brother and sister, they truly in all sense of the word were "Best friends".

I got up and walked downstairs with my head held high into the living room where the older kids were sitting, Charles, I believe was in shock and Alexys was sobbing. I began to see the destruction that would soon take place, all over again, the scene played out in front of me like a "lifetime movie". I looked around and made a choice. I remember looking up and nodding to the ceiling and I decided then and there, and I went into action in memory of my son Jarred.

I was going to take every hurt feeling of grief I had and turn it into something good. I was going to touch people with his story and reach as many people as I possibly could. I was going to obey the Holy Spirit and do exactly as instructed me to do.

I set my cell phone on the end table, then walked over and sat next to Charles. I put my arm around him because he was simply looking down. I heard my phone ring on the other side of the room. Alexys looked at me seeing that it was my Mom calling. I told her to answer it, hearing her say "Hi GG, hold on". As she was handing me the phone, I could still hear my mom speaking. I took the phone and said, "Hi Mom." She replied, "I'll just meet you at the hospital.", since she lived 10 minutes from the hospital that Jarred would likely be in, due to him living near her. In her mind this was logical versus the 45-minute drive to our house. I said, "Mom he is gone, just come here." She said again, "I will meet you at the hospital". I didn't want to say the next words but knowing my mom I had to because she would have kept insisting. I said, "Mom he is in the morgue." She didn't say a word, just hung up. I now know that she pulled her car over and called our family friends, Diane and Terry Foltz. Diane answered the phone and knowing Mom couldn't drive, she sent Terry to bring her to my house.

I don't think people understood, that I didn't lose my hearing, I lost my son. I could hear people whispering around me. They thought I was in shock because my reaction was so different this time. I remember when my mom walked in the house with Terry. I heard her ask my husband, "How is she?" He replied, "She is ok." My mother said, "She is in shock, she is not okay." Nope, I was completely at peace. I was not in shock at all; I had a new purpose in my life. Honoring the memory of my son in a way that was healthy and that helped as many people as possible.

I had peace knowing that Jarred was in his eternal home with Christ, because I showed Jarred who Christ was before he passed away. Did I hurt? Yes. Was I mad? Yes. Was this going to define me this time? NO. My foundation had changed, and in changing that, my face of grief changed. I was now experiencing something surreal and to be quite honest it was absolutely beautiful.

The day went on in a blur, my next call was to Cathy, his therapist. She answered on the first ring. "What happened?" because of the hour of the call.

I said just two words to her "COME NOW". She did not ask anything, just said "I am on my way," and hung up. She arrived about 45 minutes later. When she walked in we gave her a moment, she didn't need to be told, she simply knew. She said only one word, "How", then I explained to her the details which took Jarred's life. She then became our family's Grief therapist for the people who came in and out thru the day.

There were multiple people in and out of my house that day. By the time my mother made it to the house, most of my family knew as they were in route as well. I made it an intentional decision that I would deliver the news personally to each of his close friends. I did just that to every single friend that walked in my door. "Have a seat, I need to talk to you, He's gone, Jarred is gone." I can still close my eyes and see the faces of each person I told this to. John was first, Katie second, Britney third, it seemed to just go on and on. The last person of the day was Shiann, we had kept everything quiet until I could deliver it. She had been working so we waited for her to come. As she sat in the chair at the kitchen table looking down at the ground not saying a word. She was just shaking her head. I knew I did the right thing in delivering this personally to people Jarred was close to and cared about.

I made it thru the day without becoming angry, most of my family was there by this point. When I received the call from the organ donation person I thought to myself, "Why would you be calling me about my child who just passed away?" I didn't even know he signed up to be an organ donor, when he had gotten his Michigan Identification while living with my mom. I heard the voice again telling me "Turn hurt into Grace, do good deeds." I did just that. I called the adults into the downstairs bedroom for the dreaded call, because I wanted them to see the positivity and help that Jarred was about to show many other people. I will say that this plan backfired.

I put the phone on speaker, the call lasted 45 minutes. I am talking 45 minutes of pure agonizing questions and answers. They go thru every "Donatable" body part including skin, once they gain your permission, they go into detail how the said "part" is removed and how it will alter a viewing during a memorial. They told us how it would be "harvested" and how it will be used for someone in need.

After 45 minutes, the very last thing she said was this: "Last question, has he been incarcerated in the last 12 months?" I looked around the room and began to shake my head, because I knew he had. My oldest son's left the room, but I was honest and said yes and gave her the dates. There was silence as I sat there looking at my brother Kevin who was about to blow his top. His legs were shaking, he was shaking his head, and is face was bright red. I was more concerned with how he was about to react, as a child his nick name was "Bam Bam" for a reason. The lady said, "Mam, I am so sorry, he isn't eligible to be a donor due to this." I may have gotten a bit angry at that point, it seems that should have been the very first question. She kept me on the phone for 45 minutes to discuss harvesting my son's organs for someone in need. Just to find out that had he died TWO days later, TWO FRICKING days later. He would have been eligible to help others in need.

I mean the poor lady on the phone kept saying how sorry she was for our loss and offered us some "Donor pins" for my family to wear. Right, I mean those pins would make me feel better about spending 45 minutes on the phone discussing ways you guys were going to harvest my son's organs, bone, and skin to find out that he wasn't eligible due to a 48-hour difference in time. I am quite sure that the person who was waiting for those needs did not care that he had been in jail almost a year prior. OK, I admit that was not my most graceful moment of the day.

By the way, we never did receive those complimentary donor pins to wear showing we were organ donors, because my now deceased child was not allowed to donate due to 48-hour difference in times. So, maybe I am still a bit "salty" about that situation. If you work at a donor agency and are reading this, take note of this situation, it should have never happened. That should be the very first question that someone is asked. NOT THE LAST. The amount of unneeded grief and trauma this caused family members in that room that day, is still spoken about today. This is just my two cents regarding the situation. If you ask my brother Kevin, I am sure he would have a ton more to say on this issue.

Also, this is in no way me telling someone not to donate organs to those in need. I do think that this is a fantastic program and I know that it would have been Jarred's wishes to help as many people as he could. In fact I am a big supporter of Organ Donation, The needs for people waiting for life sustaining organs, far outweighs the people signed up for donation. What I am saying is that, there needs to be a change put in place with the order of questioning when calling loved one's families over something so sensitive. Alright back to grace.

Chapter Thirteen
My Faith is Bigger
Than my Grief

When you lose someone, you might experience the feeling of hopelessness amid being down the dark path of grief. These lies of hopelessness likely told you that you were too far gone for even GOD to find you. It was likely an impossible feat to believe that there could be a better life. How many of you have ever felt this way in your grief journey?

This story parallels what so many of us have experienced. Life can throw us into situations that feel insurmountable, that there is no way out, and that, we are so far gone it will be impossible to believe in a better life. That we are unworthy of His love.

There is a better life, one where God's power saves us from ourselves. As believers, we need to hold these truths about God firm. God has the power to pull us out of the lion's den and we can rejoice, along with Him that we are found again.

You see grief really is nothing more than trials and tribulations. The real question is "How do you respond to it?" You cannot continue to fill the holes inside with the same things that are causing said holes and expect a different result. That's the definition of Insanity as I learned at the boot camp that Jarred attended.

Choosing a better life is walking a better road, hearing, and listening to the Holy Spirit and filling those holes with scripture and faith. It is about doing the right thing each time even when no one is watching. I thank God today for filling my holes with his word.

The differences in my "Faces of Grief" with Jacob and my "Faces of Grief" with Jarred are not even parallel. If I look back on the two paths, it still shocks me even today. I had to make a conscience effort when that call came in about Jarred to choose to allow my faith to be bigger than my grief.

I have been criticized a lot for this comment since Jarred has passed away. When I say this, I am not saying that you have no Faith, what I am saying is that you must let your Faith drive your grief not the other way around. With Jarred I was able to take every pain, heartache and angry moment and use them to do good for people who were in need.

For me, taking something "bad" and using it to give "good" was how I was able to live thru the loss of my youngest biological child. When most people lose one child it cripples them, I know because it did me. But to have the opportunity to have a Do-Over, like I did, I just could not do the same thing I did before. I did not want to become the true definition of insanity again.

Faith can be an incredible comfort in times of loss and grief. Death could also cause us to question our faith, as we struggle to make sense of the death. Grief can confuse our feelings about our faith and our faith can confuse feelings about our grief. Doesn't this sound like a hamster wheel in itself?

I remember once someone saying to me, "If you believe in God there is no need to grieve." I think that it was meant with a good intention. Just like, "He is in a better place," or "It is part of God's plan." People say these things in hopes of helping the griever. This can leave believers questioning why they are still feeling the pain of grief, when someone they love is now with God.

Grief is our natural reaction to a loss. We feel a deep pain when someone we love dies. Even If we have faith that someone is in a better place or that we will see them again. This does not remove the pain that the person is gone. This does not eliminate the anger or other feelings that can come up following a death.

When a person of deep faith loses someone, it is important to remember that grief is about their own experience of loss, it is not a pain or sympathy for where their loved one is. It is perfectly acceptable to believe our loved one is in a better place, and still having the feeling of being overwhelmed from being separated from them.

We can believe in a big plan but continue to experience pain from their absence. It is not selfish to grieve, it is not a loss of faith. It is a normal reaction to a dreadful situation that can co-exist with the comfort of one's faith and spirituality.

Keeping your head above water when you experience loss is hard, especially if you don't have a firm foundation of faith. There is so much scripture in the bible that supports keeping your faith bigger than your grief. Here are a few of my favorites. I hope they help you like they did me.

> *2 Corinthians 7:10 (ESV), "For Godly grief produces a repentance that leads to salvation without regret, whereas worldly grief produces death."*

> *Philippians 4:7, "And the peace of God, which transcends all understanding, will guard your hearts and your minds in Christ Jesus."*

Colossians 1:5, "The faith and love that spring from the hope stored up for you in heaven and about which you have already heard in the true message of the gospel."

Hebrews 11:1 (NLT), "Faith is the confidence that what we hope for will actually happen; it gives us assurance about things we cannot see."

John 16:22, "So with you: Now is your time of grief, but I will see you again and you will rejoice, and no one will take away your joy."

1 Thessalonians 4:13 (ESV), "But we do not want you to be uninformed, brothers, about those who are asleep, that you may not grieve as others do who have no hope."

When I say my faith is bigger than my grief, I say this with love to people. I say this with good intentions. I know what a difference the grief journey after loss can be with and without having faith. I promise you letting your faith be bigger, allowing it to drive your grief will help heal.

Chapter Fourteen
God Given Grace

2 Corinthians 12: 9-10, "*My grace is sufficient for you, for my power is made perfect in weakness. Therefore, I will boast all the more gladly about my weaknesses, so that Christ's power may rest on me. That is why, for Christ's sake, I delight in weaknesses, in insults, in hardships, in persecutions, in difficulties. For when I am weak, then I am strong.*"

My personal story is filled with shattered pieces, questionable choices, and very ugly truths. I have done some very dark things in my life. But that same story is also filled with MAJOR comebacks and a rebirth. Guess what, yours is also! Not one of us reading this can say that they have lived a life without mistakes.

You can overcome anything if you keep your eyes fixed on the prize. Not the prize that used to come in cereal boxes. Whatever even happened to those prizes that we used to fight about getting out of our morning box of cereal as children? The prize I am talking about is the prize of your relationship with Christ. I am comforted with Joy, knowing Jarred's eternity. I am not saying that I will not grieve for my sons, I can say that my Faith is bigger than my grief now. God wants you to be comforted in that fact as well.

Being a believer is not just keeping Jesus to ourselves; it is also about keeping our eyes fixed on him even when things look gloomy. When you lose a loved one, things look dire and you feel hopeless. Look at all the things in the world through God's eyes, treat everything like it is a ministry and you cannot help but be moved to react differently to those trials and tribulations.

The influences you put yourself under is the determination of your outcomes. Broken clocks still tell the correct time two times daily right? Does that mean you do not hurt the rest of the day? Absolutely not! Even on the bad days there is a potential for a few good moments. Once you start finding the good moments, they will become more than the bad.

Proverbs 11:21, "Be sure of this:
The wicked will not go
unpunished, but those
who are righteous
will go free."

There is a lot to be said about the influence you allow. The better the influences with which we surround ourselves, the happier we will be. The more value you create, will add to our happiness. The only way to turn a bad influence into a good one is by consistently being a powerful good influence to yourself. Which, of course, requires you to challenge your own negativity and constantly win over it, and that is the hardest of tasks.

On days when I am strong enough not only to avoid being pulled into negative patterns of behavior, I have found that I have the ability to also help them avoid such negative patterns as well. On days when I am weak, I am more susceptible to negative patterns. It is quite easy when we're feeling low to spiral even lower under the influence of someone else's negative patterns. I have made this mistake a time or two, OK maybe like a million times. One thing I can be certain of is that God's given grace is always sufficient. Even when you don't feel like it is deserved.

When I trust in the sufficiency of God's Grace, I truly can be anxious for nothing. When God does intervene and rescue me, it becomes abundantly clear to me that it was not due to my brilliant strategizing, but his glorious, sufficient grace.

Chapter Fifteen
"In the Light of Eternity this Matter's"

In the light of eternity does this even matter, is one of my Pastor's favorite sayings. He says this often and each time I lean in and listen.

Please, if you take one thing away today after reading this book let it be this:

~You are not too dirty for God to clean.

~You are not too broken for God to put back together.

~You are not too far away for God to find.

~You are not too guilty for God to pardon, and

~You are utterly NOT too worthless for God to forgive.

HE ALREADY HAS.

These thoughts are just another one of Satan's tricks. He wants you to think that there is no hope or possibility that we can be forgiven, healed, and restored. Satan will try to make us feel consumed and trapped by guilt so that we do not feel worthy of God's forgiveness any longer.

We must always keep in mind that there is no place we can go that God's grace will not reach, and there is no abyss to which we can descend that God is no longer able to pull us out.

His grace is greater than all our sin. Whether we are just starting to saunter off course, already sinking, or if we are completely drowning in our sin, grace can be received. **YOU JUST HAVE TO ASK FOR IT.** People spend millions of dollars looking for the fountain of youth, but not realizing that the actual fountain of our eternal life is absolutely free.

We allow "things" to get us so wrapped up and upset, that it dictates how we live our lives...Even if we are Christians, the "temporary" things of this life can easily get out attention off Jesus. It will help if you can ask yourself, In light of eternity, what does this "temporary thing" matter?

Our world today is built on immediate gratification and living for present pleasures. If we lose the meaning of eternity and fail to see life from an eternal perspective, we lose everything important from God's point of view. To capture eternity in this life is not only to predict a future gratification, but it is to assume a present reality.

God is simply constructing character within us that will last forever. He is more concerned about our character and motives than the temporary things you attain. God looks at what is internal and invisible to others. When He looks on your heart, what does it look like?

2 Corinthians 4:17-18, "For our light and momentary troubles are achieving for us an eternal glory that far outweighs them all. So we fix our eyes not on what is seen, but on what is unseen, since what is seen is temporary, but what is unseen is eternal.

TODAY I AM THANKING JESUS THAT JARRED ACCEPTED HIS GRACE. BECAUSE OF THAT I KNOW WHERE HE RESIDES IN ETERNITY.

Chapter Sixteen
Those Daily Reminders

I would be misleading you if I told you that magically all grief will disappear. It does not. There are daily reminders that bring back the loss. But there is hope to help them to cope and heal.

When a loved one dies you will be faced with grief over your loss again and again — sometimes even years later. Feelings of grief might return on the anniversary of your loved one's death or other special days throughout the year.

Let's face it, there is always an empty seat at the table, a missing person in the family photos. Do not jump back on that hamster wheel. These feelings are not a setback; they are more a reflection that your loved one meant a lot to you. Be thankful that this reminder is still remembered. Could you imagine not remembering your loved one at all?

Reminders can be anywhere, and they are inevitable. It could be a meal, holiday, birthday, visiting a relative, or even doing something you knew they enjoyed. LITERALLY anything.

Reminders can also be a sight, sound, or smell. They can be unexpected. I know this sounds strange. Jarred had a body wash he liked that to this day when I smell it, I feel him near me in a way. In fact, I keep a small container of it in my top drawer. Because sometimes I just NEED that reminder, the opportunity to smell him again.

You can become flooded with emotions when you drive by somewhere they liked, or eat at a restaurant they ate at, or hear a favorite song. Many therapists call these reminders an "anniversary reaction", but I choose to call them "they are reminding us they are still near reaction." This does not make that feeling any easier, but instead of making it a "reaction", I have chosen to make it something positive and be "thankful" for it. Change your perspective on that feeling, Make it a blessing not a curse.

The problem with these reminders is that they are unpredictable. So be prepared when you begin to feel those intense trigger reactions.

For me, seeing how badly I handled it when Jacob died, versus how I handled Jarred's death, I still do not understand how my husband stood by me. It was that awful. We had a lot of healing to do for our marriage for sure after this.

I can remember having angry outbursts, anxiety, crying spells, depression, no energy, guilt, pain, and trouble sleeping when Jacob died. I simply did not with Jarred because my foundation was different. I remember having some angry outbursts, I still do sometimes to be completely transparent. I also gained the weight back that I lost after Jacob passed away. But I am working on that still.

These feelings will also provoke powerful memories of your loved one. Sometimes you can remember things in detail. But remembering those feelings can also provoke so much unneeded trauma on your loved ones that are alive as well. If you change your perspective on the outcome it will help you.

Even years after a loss, you may continue to become triggered when faced with reminders of your grief. Keep healing, continue to take steps to cope with reminders of your loss. It's not always easy, but it is always a choice. I failed so badly when Jacob died, I didn't let myself feel any of it. In return that destroyed almost every reminder whether good or bad that I had. It wasn't until much later that I could feel joy over those small reminders. I can now and I am thankful for that.

With Jarred things were quite different, in fact it was somewhat beautiful in all ways shape and form. I turned it all into good and reached as many as I could. There is still a specific reminder that I get every year that just makes me laugh. Jarred was a jokester of sorts. One year he decided to throw a bottle of open Dawn dish soap in a local city fountain that sits in the middle of town. There were bubbles everywhere, in fact running down the parking lot into the road.

The local news covered it, there are photos everywhere on this. I get tagged in them every year, in fact occasionally someone will do it again just in remembrance of him. Ok, it is not entirely appropriate, but it makes me laugh each time.

Some things I still try to do to cope are:

~**Make time to sit with your feelings:** Ignoring them might seem like a good way to get rid of feelings, but evading could have the opposite effect. Think of your feelings like a volcano that is live, it is going to erupt at some point in time. Let that lava flow in a healthy way.

~**Distract:** Do something you enjoy, find a new hobby. Sometimes finding a bit of joy doing something different can help you refocus your perspective.

~**Interact don't hide:** Spending time with others reminds you to cherish other social connections and relationships.

~**Give back:** Donate time to people who need it. Do things in remembrance of your loved one.

~**Allow it:** It is okay to be sad and feel the loss. As you celebrate special memories, you might find yourself both laughing and crying at the same time.

The key is to keep going, even when it does not seem possible. A close friend and sponsor to Jarred called Billy P, used to tell me when Jarred was both in active addiction and after he passed away, "Keep on Keeping on."

In reality we all have those moments where we feel like we cannot go on for another day. Especially when we are dealing with hard daily reminders of those who we lost. It is normal to struggle with how to keep going. Do not beat yourself up if you screw up, it is bound to happen. If you get stuck there this will only discourage you further. Pick yourself back up and remember that perfection is not the goal. The goal is to stay the course. Sometimes we will fall, just don't stay there. Brush yourself off and "Keep on Keeping on". Every time we keep going even when we do not want to you are one step closer to where you want to be.

> ***Ephesians 2:10, "For we are
> God's handiwork, created in
> Christ Jesus to do good works,
> which God prepared in advance
> for us to do."***

Chapter Seventeen
That "Awakening" Grief

Even years after a loss, you might continue to feel sadness when you are confronted with reminders of your loved one's death. As you continue healing, take steps to cope with the reminders of your loss. This is hard sometimes because you never know when things will trigger you.

I remember once sitting in a McDonald's parking lot waiting for someone who ran in to go to the restroom. A young boy walked out, and he was wearing a beanie hat, it nailed me, instant tears. I remembered Jarred about a month prior to his death walking out of a McDonalds shirtless, in torn jeans and a beanie hat. I could not understand what he did with his sweatshirt, I know he walked in there with a purple Marilyn Monroe hoodie on. When he got into the car with his chicken nuggets. I said "UMMM where is your shirt?" He simply replied, "There was an older lady inside that looked cold and liked my sweatshirt, so I gave it to her." He literally gave this woman the shirt off his back. My faith was again renewed in him this day.

But this did not stop me from having a trigger reaction after he passed away when the young man walked out of the McDonalds.

Knowledge is power, be prepared, knowing the possibility of this will help you overcome these triggers and stay ahead of it. It is going to happen; you just never really know when.

Plan things on the days you know you might be triggered. For me it was doing good deeds for others that kept my head out of the clouds and from falling into the depression I knew I could easily fall back into.

I like to start new traditions, not in place of the old ones we had with the boys but add a new tradition to the old one to make it "whole". This puts a different perspective on it.

Remember it is ok to feel a range of emotions and feel the loss you had. But please do not be so consumed in that loss that you forget to experience the joy and happiness you shared with your loved one. When you celebrate special times, you might find yourself laughing and feeling a sense of peace. Each piece of Joy you experience needs to be celebrated, a little celebration of joy will help when you are feeling down and falling back under that water.

Lastly, PRAY....Pray going into the day, during the day and at the end of the day. When you know you have a pending trigger or feel that trigger coming on, PRAY first then allow yourself to feel. Sometimes just talking to God out loud about the feeling you are having can change your whole perspective completely. I often have private conversations with God when I need direction. That is ok....Ask for it.

Here are a couple prayers I use when I get triggered or feel hopeless. They helped me, maybe they will help you too.

"God help me not to sit in my own grief and anger, but in everything I do let me look to you, so that you can direct my words, thoughts, and actions. In Jesus' Name, Amen."

"God, I need you now, hurry and help me. Take this all-consuming pain and grief that I feel right now. Take it from me and heal my broken heart and bind up these wounds. Amen."

If you make God the center of your core life, He will help heal and restore you. Your relationship with God should not be put on a shelf to get dusty until something tragic happens. It should not be the bible on the shelf collecting dust, there is nothing better than a well broken in bible. I am talking where the page ends that you flip thru are broken into your own fingertips. To this day I smile when my fingers hit the grooves of my bible, especially when it lands on Micah.

Your relationship with God should be front and center 24/7/365. God requires full custody of you, not just weekend visitation. God did not come by and kick us when we were down, he extended his hand down to help us up. Its free will if you take his help.

When Jesus died on the cross his blood was shed for the penalty of our sins. The gift of God is eternal life in Christ. Do not make this your free pass, in doing the wrong thing, if you understand what God went thru for us, you want to strive to rise above all grief and anger to be your true whole self. That awakening grief is going to happen, multiple times even. Pray it out.

John 16:22,

"So with you: Now is your time of grief,

But I will see you again and you will rejoice,

And no one will take away your joy."

Chapter Eighteen
Grief is a
NON-JUDGEMENT ZONE

Every person who has experienced a loss grieves differently than the next person. It really is as unique as their own fingerprint. In your home make it where "grief is a nonjudgement zone". Meaning do not judge someone else for their grief process.

Grief is what is going on inside of us, while mourning is what we do on the outside. THESE ARE TWO SEPARATE THINGS. Grief is a battle within yourself, in your soul, while mourning is what others see you do to process your loss.

Each person in your inner circle/family will handle this differently. If children are involved, they grieve a different way as well. One common thing is this, people who are grieving do want their grief to be acknowledged. The world today has poured a bottle of hand sanitizer on grief, to kill off all the bad mojos. It makes me sad that when someone loses someone it has become so regulated, almost cookie cutter expectations.

If you lose an immediate family member, most are given just three days off work and expected to go back to work and "poof" the world is okay again. In a way, that causes self-isolation. You get up, go to work, go home from work, eat dinner, go to bed then get up and do it all over again. So, in all reality there has become less occasions for loved ones and people inside your inner circle to see you and witness your mourning and grief.

I had someone ask me once, "Angela, how long do you think these feelings last?" I simply replied snarky "I don't know, how long you think they will be dead?" Again, Grief should be a NON-JUDG-MENT ZONE.

Families who are going thru the grief process need to understand that "time simply does not heal all." In fact, in my experience, once you feel healed something at some point and time will trigger them. Walk thru this, not around it. Do not let anyone tell you how to feel, each feeling has a different face to each person.

The worse feeling is the feeling of judgment and feeling like family members and friends are judging your grief journey. I had a tough time with this. I always felt like people were judging my thought process and how I was handling things. What I do not think that they understood is that no matter what, there is always an empty seat at the table, an empty space in a picture being taken and that Christmas stocking to be hung for someone who is no longer with us. Guess what, this will not change, there is always that spot that you will envision your loved one's face. It is hard to not get hurt or angry each time. It is extremely hard. Do I hang the stocking or don't I hang the stocking, etc. etc. People judge you either way, so you might as well do what you want to do anyway.

Those "first" after you lose a loved one are hard. The first Holidays, birthdays and those special days. "DO YOU", don't become a cookie cutter. To this day I hang my son's stockings, I still have their pictures up for all to see and we still continue to put their special ornaments on the Christmas tree. Don't let anyone tell you that you are doing it wrong, unless of course you are doing it like I did with Jacob, because let's face it, that was terribly wrong.

Open up communication with your family, discuss the "firsts". We find peace now each time a special moment passes that brings us memories of my son's. We engage in open conversation about it, bringing us joy rather than being stuck in sorrow.

Most of the time people have the best intentions when "thinking" that "they" are "helping" you deal with your grief. Those who know you should not judge you or think your grieving wrong, unless of course it is to the point of your own demise and/or your families like it was for Jacob's passing. Grief does not simply begin on day one of the passing and end on a certain date.

Some have said, it takes about a year to grieve a loved one. I say that is a bunch of bull. Do people just think that at day 366, you magically wake up with rainbows and unicorns on your heart and brain? NO, it is a constant battle, some days are better than others. But it is an ongoing choice to choose, wide or narrow. It does lessen over time, but it is always near and easily triggered.

You cannot compare your grief with anyone else's grief even if in the same family. People should not judge you for the way you grieve your loved one and vice versa. One thing I can promise you is that those who are in a very dark place won't be ready to hear about hope, and how things will get better because they're at the beginning of their book of grief. Their grief is too severe to allow for any other feeling other than that. They just want the darkness of their grief to be seen and acknowledged. Acknowledge it, let them know that you love them.

Don't be judgmental and make them feel like they are doing something wrong. EVEN IF THEY ARE in your opinion, handle that with caution. I know that my husband held it together so well when

Jacob died, that no one knew, but I don't know if I would have been real receptive if someone did try to talk to me about my behavior at that time. In looking back that was a desperate situation, he should have pushed me to get the help I needed. But I don't blame him, for this.

It was really about my foundation needing to be replaced with Christ. This opened my heart to a different way and a different method with healing from losing my son's. It's hard to understand how the grieving person feels when they are being judged for their process.

It's like taking a potato peeler and peeling off the top layer of your healing wounds. I know you are likely cringing right now reading this. Most of us have caught our hand while peeling potatoes, so you understand that feeling. I'm NOT sorry for saying this, don't be a potato peeler. I can hear my mother right now saying, "Angela Marie".

Chapter Nineteen
Childhood Heartache

Children grieve a bit differently than adults. Same type of feelings simply different ways of coping. I have had the opportunity to see how "MY" grief reaction shaped their grief process. Again, this is not cookie cutter, it will not be the same for everyone. Sadly this is my experience I missed all of these reactions when Jacob passed away, I was available and more in-tune with my children when we lost Jarred. Some of the behaviors I noticed were anxiety, fear, anger, dislike for school, isolation, night-mares, depression, taking on adult responsibilities, self-medicating and acting out in negative ways. Children will not just sit down and talk to parents about these feelings when they know you are struggling also.

Remember, children need ongoing attention, support, and encouragement so they know what they are going thru is normal. Even if as the parent we do not quite understand it I assure you it is quite real to them. Also, keep in mind that grief will continue to reappear with children.

It is difficult to get into your child's world when you feel like your world is falling apart. Please take this as a warning from me. **DON'T LET THAT HAPPEN.** You could lose a part of them you will not get back. Especially if it is their sibling that has passed away. Parents (myself included) tend to focus on the late child and not the alive child. You talk, eat, and breathe your deceased child.

This will send the wrong message to your children. It could make them feel like they need to behave in a way to gain attention, usually this is shown in negative behaviors that will also disrupt the grief process of your home. Or worse, send your child down a road of their own destruction that you may never have the opportunity to get a "Do-Over" with. Because let's face it, attention is attention whether positive or negative.

A lot of times, children act out because they are responding in a normal way to an abnormal situation. This has upset them to the point that they are having a hard time managing their emotions. Don't we as parents do the same thing sometimes?!

Those social media memories pop up and get shared and conversations circle around the loss. This will leave your alive children feeling alone. Do not be so focused on the dead that you forget to be present for your children that are here waiting. I failed this miserably when Jacob passed away, I thank God I was a different person when we loss Jarred.

There are significant long-term effects on childhood grief. I cannot preach that enough. So I will say this again, "**THERE ARE SIGNIFICANT LONG-TERM EFFECTS ON CHILDHOOD GRIEF.**" This includes mental health issues, substance abuse, PTSD and behavioral problems. This is just to name a few I have experienced. I am sure I missed many more behaviors.

You do not want to support your children wrong in this, I pray you do NOT get a Do-Over like I did. Get inside their world and meet them where they are at, not where you want them to be. This could change at any given time. If you have multiple children in the same home as we do, all I can say is hang on for the ride because it is going to get turbulent. The kind of turbulence that is going to make you not understand if it is day or night, if it is hot or cold etc. Each child will grieve differently. So, hey mom and dad, have fun putting yourself back together while keeping your kids together also. It can be done; you have to make a conscience effort to make your faith bigger than your grief.

Learn to heal and cope as a unit. If you are not able to, get them to speak to your pastor, a therapist or someone they trust. This may be the most difficult part of your own grieving process as well. When parents see their children hurt, it hurts us as well. We naturally want to fix it and make it better.

But be cautious to not make our "adult" problems, their problems.

When someone dies, it affects the way the family functions as a whole. Every relationship in the family may shift. So children won't only mourn the person who died, but also the change in the family environment and the changed family relationships members may play. That change won't only affect them in the now, but in the years ahead. One of the most important factors in how children are affected by loss is the support these children receive from parents, siblings, extended family, and friends.

Children need to be given the opportunity to experience and express their feelings. They need support and encouragement to understand what happened, identify their feelings, and support the memory of the person they lost.

Remember that you have to care for yourself, before you can care for you child who is grieving. You simply cannot fill from an empty tap. Caring for yourself after a death is important. Pay attention to your feelings and lean on loved ones or talk to a mental health provider. Get enough sleep, eat a healthy diet and stay active. This will enable you to care for your child and serve as a role model for how to cope.

Chapter Twenty
Self Care

Self-care is difficult under normal circumstances, but when you are grieving and mourning a loved one, it is near non-existent. TRUST ME. I get it, I remember taking a shower when I needed to bawl my eyes out so no one would hear me crying. Little did I know they all knew that was what I was doing.

When Jacob passed, I was 142 pounds. During my destruction, I maxed out at 218. Keep in mind, I am only 5'1 tall. I then lost all the weight in 2015 and got back down to my normal weight (ish). I did this thanks to the book by Jasinda Wilder called *Big Girls Do It Running*. Then guess what, I gained every pound of it back plus 10 pounds when Jarred died. Guess what book I am re-reading, I will get there again, the program is pretty simple to follow. When Jarred died, I picked up all the "bad foods and sugar" again. People bring food to help feed your family, I didn't care and just ate it. Self-care is hard when you're grieving, there is no doubt about this.

Even after I became healthier in my mind and found my faith, I still struggled with self-care, in fact I still do. Don't all mothers?

Self-care is more than just eating right, getting enough sleep, being kind to yourself, getting up and get moving, drinking more water, etc. I mean, those are great, they need to be practiced. When you are grieving there is a whole new level of needs for self-care that people just do not think of. Here are a few of my favorites. They may be a bit unconventional. I get that, but clearly you can already tell that I have done things a bit differently.

~Take a walk in the woods, so you can scream and cry,

~Get fresh air so you can breathe deep,

~ Get some sun, life can get dark when you are grieving.

~Lay outside if it is raining (Trust me, sad people love the rain, makes us feel like we're not crying alone).

~Practice patience, forgiveness, and gratitude.

~Blare worship music, listen and sing the words.

~Pray, Have conversations with God...A LOT.

~Volunteer. Do good deeds for others.

~Garden. Either veggies or flowers.

~Write. Put your thoughts on paper.

~Did I mention prayer?

It is absolutely okay to have a bad day. There are still days I go to bed wearing the same pajamas I woke up in. Having a bad day is okay if you do not get stuck there. With Jacob I was stuck there and could not move past it for a long time. With Jarred from day one I would NOT allow myself to be stuck in that destructive mindset.

The stress associated with grieving can actually affect every aspect of your own being, your mental, physical, emotional and spiritual self. It only takes a short time for you to use your energy up, deplete your resources and become overwhelmed and exhausted from your own stress. It is important to remember to continue to practice self-care in order to continue to fill your depleted mental, physical, emotional and spiritual self-bucket.

Understand that grieving is really hard work. It requires a great deal of energy and is exhausting. Especially when most go back to work and try to keep not only their job together but their home as well. It is important to ask for, and accept, help from those close to you. It is really hard to accept help when you're falling apart.

Other people care and want to help you, but these same people do not know what to specifically offer in fear of making you angry. If they offer to help you clean your house, you're likely to think that they are in the thought process that your house is dirty, if they offer to bring a meal, you're likely to think that they don't think you can cook. Really in all reality they are just trying to help you with self-care.

It is immensely helpful to know who will listen and be supportive. Sharing your story out loud is one key to healing. Sharing your story can give you a sense that you are not alone in this journey.

If you have ever listened to someone talk about their story it might remind you that "Oh, someone else has been through that, too? I thought it was just me!" You can sometimes find some similarities that could help comfort you. Remember every story shared is a chance to make someone feel less alone also. You never know, you may have something that someone else is waiting to and needing to hear.

There is no right way to tell your story – it's yours to tell, so share it in the way that works best for you. Some find it easy just sitting down with your best friend, or family. Maybe writing it will help, even if you don't publish that like I am doing. Remember your story is your testimony, it could be the catalyst to your healing. It could also be the catalyst in helping someone else heal as well. One of the most powerful ways of being inspirational to others is by using the one tool you have that no one else has – your own story.

Chapter Twenty-One
Firm Foundation

Following my spiritual path was tough for me, partly because of what I screwed up in my own life, partly because of what I screwed up in my children's life and partly because let's face it....... IT'S WORK. The honest to God best way to describe this is that you must make the "INTENT" a full-time job. I know, like I really need another job, I am already a mother, wife, mentor, advocate...But it really does come if you begin to work it. I am hoping that you do not allow your grief to become your foundation, but if you do that is ok. God does not mind the timing because his timing is perfect.

The hardest part for me was allowing God to be my general contractor. Allowing him to completely bull doze and wipe my foundation clean down to the dirt.

I had to allow God to level the ground before even trying to rebuild my foundation.

Doing this is exhausting, mentally, physically, and emotionally.

Think of it this way. When you decide to build a house from the ground up, do you look for a level/flat piece of land or one that already has things built on it?

Either way, you know you must build from the ground up. You must get rid of things in the way of this, whether it be trees, roots, buildings. So, think of this in the route of getting rid of any Hurts, Habits or Hang ups. **LEVEL THAT FOUNDATION.**

When you look at society in our world today, there is so much missing, and when looking at the grand scheme of the world that missing puzzle piece is "God", "Faith", "Grace" and "Kindness."

Most people's foundation is riddled with Doubt, Confusion, Bad Relationships, Habits, Mistrust and Sin. How can you expect God to rebuild that when you are not willing to pull it up by the roots? Because it is a root that will spread and build within you a big old 'Negative garden of chaos and dysfunction." **LEVEL THAT FOUNDATION.**

I have now learned to use a thought process that is scripture based and easy for me to understand and teach. Let me take you to:

Philippians 4:8, "Finally, brothers and sisters, whatever is true, whatever is noble, whatever is right, whatever is pure, whatever is lovely, whatever is admirable—if anything is excellent or praiseworthy— think about such things."

When I start experiencing inner turmoil and begin to struggle with a thought process, whether it be grief, parenting, relationships, faith etc., I ask myself this, "Does this line up with Scripture?" If it does not then **I LEVEL IT.**

Every thought, behavior and reaction you have try to use this method, even if you need to write Philippians 4:8 on every mirror of your house.

~Is this true?

~Is this Honorable?

~Is this pure?

~Is this lovely?

~Is this commendable?

~Is there any excellence to it?

If you answer NO to any of the above, then **LEVEL IT.** Buy that bulldozer (Bible) and **LEVEL IT.**

The toxicity of the "NO's" will stop you from growing in faith. There is no way around this, it will prevent the Lord from rebuilding your foundation and the life he expects and wants for you.

To build that strong foundation, we need to "Allow and Let" God dig deep down and purge out our junk. Keep in mind while you dig a hole sometimes things seep in from around you. Make sure that you are not allowing yourself to be vulnerable to "Satan's attacks". Make sure that you are filling that hole with "Faith and Scripture".

I remember growing up when my grandmother used to brush my hair out. Mind you, I have very kinky curly hair - the kind that people pay big money for and I pay big money to relax. Well, when my grandmother would brush my hair I would sit and yell "Ouch, Ouch, Ouch." She used to say to me. "Being beautiful can sometimes be painful Angela Marie." I never quite got that until I allowed God to bulldoze my foundation. It was painful, hard and eye opening. But at the end is an incredibly beautiful result of the pain.

Every beautiful flower begins with a seed planted in dirt, then forms roots and sprouts. It then will die if you do not water and fertilize it properly. Make sure that your worth is where it needs to be and that begins with the foundation of your life.

Chapter Twenty-Two
My Today

My life today is so much different than the beginning of the book. It is painful to see the journey and the havoc that a lot of it created. It really was so simple, yet due to circumstances, Redo's and surrender it was made so much more difficult than it needed to be.

My journey, although hard, painful with multiple train derailments, some even being head-on collisions, I can now say "God gave me grace".

My today is quite different, I want to live every day for Christ and know that if I were to be taken home today, I know where I would be. I am teaching my younger children this as well.

I still fail daily in being a wife and mother. God knows that is fact. The difference is "Grace".

My relationships with my older children will be forever changed due to their upbringing. But that is a work in progress.

I can say that my daughter Alexys and I are remarkably close, she has found her faith and resonates that now in her daily life. My son Charles believes but does not currently practice in the sense of going to church weekly, it is a work in progress. He has had a ton of loss in his short life in losing his two brothers and grandfather. His foundation of Grief is much different. This has really shaped him as an adult. My son Robert is married with two sons of his own, their faith I believe is evolving, I know that the boys do go to church sometimes, and they allow me to take them on days that I may have them, usually when camping in the summertime. Gavin is married as well, he and his wife have beliefs, however they are not tied to one religion. In fact, they are not religious really at all, but they do discuss their thoughts on what happens when they die and such. So, they do have beliefs but would not classify them as religious. Life was definitely different for my older children growing up, this is my fault. I am still going to continue to plant those seeds of faith in them. All it takes is one to sprout. Look what it did for me.

Our younger children in the home are being brought up totally different. They are being brought up with strong faith. They attend church weekly, even participating either in worship on stage, sound or videography, or helping teach in the programs. We homeschool our children now as well, we keep their circle pretty small in fact. In return I am sure that their children are going to be brought up quite different because their foundations were broken when we took placement of them, so we had to Level their ground and rebuild that.

In a different way of course, due to abuse and neglect in child welfare. We have shown them how to "Bulldoze" their foundation and rebuild it with Christ. What we have found is that when we take in these kids, we can core them (bulldoze) and fill them with Christ, and it heals.

After seeing the way that God has worked in our lives with the children we can honestly say "When you help a child it helps, but when you help a child and lead them to Christ it heals."

My husband and I are still learning to do this, together. We have built a life that we do not need or want a vacation from. We have a life that revolves around God, Our children, and what we call our inner circle. We break bread at our table as a family nightly, have our traditional homemade pizza and movie night on Fridays, Church, and soup dinners on Sundays. We all participate in outreach in our community, except for the Trafficked children, I am solo on that due to safety. But in all we are a unit, a well-oiled machine of sorts.

We are overly cautious of the "yoke" we allow in our home; we do not like scrambled eggs. Meaning, if you are not from our same yoke in faith you are not in our home at a level where our inner circle partakes. It only takes one bad yoke to disrupt the dozen eggs. We are very protective of our inner circle. It is ok to protect that Foundation that you have fought to build.

Scripture stated in:

> **2 Corinthians 6:14, "Do not be yoked together with unbelievers. For what do righteousness and wickedness have in common? Or what fellowship can light have with darkness?"**

Does this mean we do not minister and reach those who do not have the same or no Faith? NO, we are cautious with our inner peace in our home. Keeping this mentality according to scripture has really made our house function as God has intended. Sometimes separating yoke is hard, sometimes it hurts having to do it. But if you follow God's scripture and follow the words that he gave it will honestly work itself out.

I have found the closer we stay true to this path of "yoke" the better that our house runs. At this point our younger children will tell us themselves when they feel that someone isn't equally yoked. This is their foundation now.

I know this book took you all over the place and back again, it lost me a time or too as well. But to keep it true to my late children, I felt their stories needed to be told in a way that showed the "why", not just their "when". It was a process that you the reader needed to understand and go thru, to better understand when hearing my story of faith.

I am just an ordinary everyday mom with no special initials behind my name. I am no expert on faith. This is just my story; it makes me an expert of grief sadly. I miss my boys greatly, BUT I am so blessed that God gave me Grace and a Do-Over to figure my own foundation out; in doing so he has helped us help well over 50 children to date. This is a working number that is changing daily with every call and need that comes in. I hope that you can take a little bit away from it, whether that be healing, faith, surrender or just learning how to be the director of your own troubled youth. Whatever that may be, make sure that it is well in your soul and it is done with Grace, Love and Dignity and trust God's ways always. The rules are written and have been for around 3400 years.

Chapter Twenty-Three
Legacy of the Red Bowtie

Jarred loved "Red Bow-Ties". It has really become symbolic. The day of Jarred's memorial, his friends did something called #bowtiesforjarred. Everyone came in bow-ties. It was an amazing sight to see. In fact, you could not find one to purchase in the surrounding areas, they were sold out. It was interesting to see everyone sporting something in direct memory of him.

We decided to keep that symbology in things we did in remembrance of him.

We have done a lot in memory of Jarred. We currently live in the same area we did when he passed away and he was well known. I knew when I started grieving for Jarred I needed to listen and do exactly as the Holy Spirit directed me to do. I needed to do good deeds, help people, and reach as many people as possible with his story. I started to look at everything I did as a ministry in memory of Jarred.

The more I began to share his story, the more I saw that he was still helping people even in his death. Here are a few of the outreach things that we do in his memory.

We moved the closet to a new location, and it is called "Jarred's Bow Tie closet." We service people in need along with members of Michigan Department of Health and Human Services (MDHHS) for foster children. We offer clothing and personal care items just like Jarred did out of our basement.

We adopted a 3-mile stretch of highway in our hometown in memory of Jarred and we maintain it. We do clean up's multiple times a year and people from all over come to help assist us. To date we have cleaned up 324 bags of garbage.

We visited an orphanage in Honduras taking needed supplies of books and school supplies to donate. Of course, each book had "In memory of Jarred" written in them with a Bow Tie.

While in Honduras, we met a gentleman who was a Pastor with his own church. My church, along with my family, adopted them in sorts and did a donation drive for him to be able to rebuild his church and construct their own "Jarred's Bow Tie closet."

Child trafficking is real in our world today sadly. I continue to work on the front line to help combat and help girls get out of this cycle of sexual slavery and exploitation. I help connect with services in the community and/or moving to a safe location. I speak and train people on the signs of Human Trafficking and internet safety. #SPARROW #GHOST.

I became a CASA, which is a Court appointed special advocate for children in the foster care system. If you are interested visit https://nationalcasa-gal.org/

We have "Bow Tie meal cards" that we have given out to people in need that they can use to access food in the community, via select restaurants and service providers.

We continue to help children, teens, and adults in need. I honestly never understood how far connections Jarred made in the community would be needed as I travel this world without him.

In short, get yourself a "Red Bow Tie" and each time you look at it think about the journey of my son. You can and will learn to live again.

#gooddeedsforjarred

Trust it, Trust His Ways and Trust His Name!

THE END

If you enjoyed this book and think it will help others, please take a few moments to write a review on your favorite store, and refer it to your friends.

What's Next?

From Darkness to Light, my Wicca story

Daily devotional for Grieving parents

Connect With Me?

www.Angelamrodgers.com

For speaking engagements, please email:

Contact@Angelamrodgers.com

FB: AngelaMRodgers

If you would like your book personalized, please send personalization instructions along with a Pre-Paid self-addressed return envelope to:

Author Angela Rodgers

PO box 544

Owosso, MI 48867